To
Paul & Laura
Gamper
from

[signature]

Thanks for spending the Sabbath with us!
Be Blessed.
5/4/2014

From the Author of Theo-Economics

WEALTH

It's In Your Worship Not Your Works

Dr. Roland J. Hill

Wealth: It's In Your Worship Not Your Works

Copyright © 2012 by Roland J. Hill

Helping Hands Press
P.O. Box 380941
Duncanville, Texas 75138
www.helpinghandspress.com

All Scripture quotations, unless otherwise noted, are taken from *The Holy Bible, English Standard Version,* copyright © 2001 by *Crossway Bibles* and *The Message Bible* © 2002 Eugene H. Peterson.

All rights reserved. No part of this work may be reproduced or transmitted in any form or by any means, electronic or mechanical, including photocopying and recording, or by any information storage or retrieval system, except as may be expressly permitted by the 1976 Copyright Act or in writing from the publisher. Requests for permission should be addressed to Helping Hands Press, P. O. Box 380941, Duncanville, Texas 75138.

Edited by Kenneth Hall, Patricia Humphrey, Susie Hill
Cover Design by Roland J. Hill and Madelein Terreros
Book Layout by Tammy G. Prieto

ISBN 1-889390-14-3

Dedicated

to

the late Dr. Franklin S. Hill, Sr.
and
Mrs. Lucille E. Hill
My parents, who taught me early in life
the joy and benefits of Sabbath observance.

ACKNOWLEDGEMENTS

This book evolved out of a series of sermons preached at the Living Waters Worship Center in Duncanville, Texas, several years ago. When I was finally able to take a Sabbatical to write, my plans were to simply edit my sermons and put them in book form, but God had a different plan. Instead, God instructed me to use the sermons as a foundation for my writing while He down loaded fresh new concepts that would take a deeper look at wealth creation. So, I must first give God praise for the ideas that have developed into this book. They are not mine. I thank God for entrusting me with His thoughts. Then, I want to thank the Living Waters Worship Center, my church family. This precious group of saints permitted me every week to mount the pulpit and preach as God inspired me. They encouraged me to keep digging for a deeper understanding of God and encouraged me to write and distribute my discoveries to the world. This loving group of believers permitted and funded my Sabbatical so I could have time on the mouto write. While I am no longer their senior pastor, they still honor my wife and me as their spiritual mother and father, and for that we will be ever grateful. Thank you Living Waters.

I want to thank also Leighton Holley, former president of the Texas Conference of Seventh-day Adventists for his wisdom in permitting me to take a Sabbatical. I could not have completed this project without the professional, gracious, and joyous help of Mario Ledezmo, Ivan Cruz, Eric Manzano, Doug Denny, Tammy G. Prieto, and Madelein Terreros, all members of the Texas Conference Print Shop team. Thank you. I will be

ACKNOWLEDGEMENTS

forever grateful for Weimar Institute. Being there while writing was like two weeks in heaven. Special thanks to my son and daughter in the ministry, Marlon and Shurla Perkins, whom God sent to pastor Living Waters. I also owe a debt of gratitude to Pastor Perkins for his encouragement and belief that this project has enormous potential for the Kingdom. Thank you, Elisa and Russell Thompson, LaShunda and Randy Rhaming for stepping up to the plate and directing the marketing for this book.

Family is important and I thank God for my sister, Terry, and her husband Michael Harris, and my brothers, Franklin, Bryon, and Hallerin. Then there are my children, my son Mian Hill, daughter Sonia and her husband Derrick Meadow with my three beautiful granddaughters. To have their love and respect means a lot to me. I dedicated this book to my parents and every day I understand better why. They provided me the DNA, training, and encouragement that has made me the preacher, teacher, father, husband, man of God, and writer that I am. I miss them greatly and look forward to spending Sabbath with them in eternity.

Finally, I've been blessed with a great wife, Susie. Words can't express my gratitude and appreciation for her support, encouragement, insights, and hard work, given not just for this project, but throughout our ministry. We are a team and this book is a reflection of that teamwork. I love you Susie, and I want the world to know it. Thanks!

- Dr. Roland J. Hill

TABLE OF CONTENTS

Acknowledgements 4

Preface 9

What Leaders Are Saying 12

Why This Book? 20

Introduction 22

Chapter One - The Mother Lode 27

Chapter Two - The Secret & Fable One 37

Chapter Three - The Law of Dependence & Fable Two 49

Chapter Four - The Bank of Heaven 63

Chapter Five - Wealth: It's in Your Worship 81

Chapter Six - You Are Job 97

Chapter Seven - The Divine Law of Attraction
                           & Fable Three 121

Conclusion 143

Glossary of Terms 145

Endnotes 147

About the Author 149

PREFACE

Wealth: It's In Your Worship Not Your Works, by Dr. Roland Hill, is a book whose time has come. This book is a fresh approach to the Sabbath. In it Dr. Hill presents clear and compelling reasoning on the true source of wealth. It is motivational and inspirational, and a read not only for ministers, but for every person who is serious about discovering, uncovering, and tapping into their God given, unlimited source of wealth.

Dr. Hill makes it plain that he is not presenting a "how to" book on the accumulation of dollars, euros, gold, diamonds or real estate. He is fundamentally challenging the way Christians think about themselves in connection with worship as a source of wealth. Hill states his purpose, "__The truth about wealth is tangled up, tied up, and hidden in the undergrowth of non-biblical philosophies many of which are unsuitable for Christian consumption. This book is the clearing in the jungle." And truly, Dr. Hill demonstrates just that. With the precision of a liturgical scalpel, he cuts away the diseased thinking apparatus that has elevated the "Protestant Work Ethic," the "Pull Yourself Up by Your Own Bootstraps" philosophy, and the fallacious Prosperity Gospel ideologies exposing them to the light of biblical truth.

Almost immediately in this ground-breaking work, Dr. Hill points his readers to the true locus of wealth–the seventh day Sabbath which connects us to our Creator. Hill states, "That, while wealth may include material possessions, ultimately wealth is about value, God's value of man and what man's values in the world." He points out that God assigned value to His Creation, and to His relationship to His Creation, ultimately assigning value to His relationship to humanity. It is in the Sabbath rest that God renews and develops what He values, thus, true wealth is in our worship, not in our works. Hill states, "In a real sense then, God alone assigns value, He is the quintessence of all wealth. Therefore in God, not in the created world, we find worth, the essence of true wealth. Evidenced in the order of the creation is God's statement of value for the human family. God created the world, then; man, not man, then the world."

True worship reconnects man with his Creator, who re-infuses him with value. It is in coming to God in the setting of true worship, recognizing and proclaiming His awesomeness in the context of our nothingness–and therefore our dependence on Him for all things–that we are reminded of the source of true value.

Dr. Hill explains the law of self-interest versus the law of dependence. Twenty-first century people forget they are already created in God's image and are therefore wealthy and are of value. Living by the law of self-interest, they look for increasingly more opportunities to gain material goods, thinking that possessing things indicates wealth and value. The law of dependence reveals that as we remember our Creator God as the Source of value and depend on Him, we know that we are esteemed and valued because He made us. This truth is bound up in the Sabbath Rest. God's gracious command to keep the Sabbath is not for His good, but for ours.

Dr. Hill draws on a parable (read the book to discover which one) and incidents in the history of God's people, such as the 40 year miracle of the Manna, or of God's delivery of it and Israel's gathering it during their sojourn in the wilderness, demonstrating the irrevocable truth of our need to acknowledge the Law of Dependence.

This book has the potential to re-align the thinking of every serious Christian regarding value and worth. Reading this excellent book will refocus, reenergize and re-enthuse the Christian Church.

- Dr. Ricardo Graham
President - Pacific Union Conference of Seventh-day Adventists,
Westlake, CA

WHAT LEADERS ARE SAYING:

"Dr. Hill has done a masterful job of focusing attention on what really matters when it comes to the subject of wealth and its value and how we should approach the study of wealth creation. He directs the reader's attention away from cash, stocks, property, etc., to things of eternal value. He states that the pursuit of wealth boils down to dependence. The ultimate question is, "What or who will we depend on?" Since the Sabbath establishes God as Creator and Sustainer of all life, then value comes in our worship rather than our works."

- Larry Moore
President, Southwestern Union Conference of Seventh-day Adventists, Burleson, TX

"There is no doubt that the Spirit of God has delivered this most timely message to God's people by means of this wonderful work which encourages us all to realign ourselves with God's will. Dr. Hill artistically brings out how the Sabbath is the centerpiece of the Law of Dependence upon God our Maker and Sustainer. We, much like the Israelites, are so often not only oppressed by the gods of this world, but also sadly blinded to our true potential. Finally, personally I loved the concept that there is no excuse for a non-productive life. You and I have the unique and solemn task of validating God's Word to a parched world. Thank you Dr. Roland Hill."

- Carlos Craig
President, Texas Conference of Seventh-day Adventists, Alvarado, TX

"I thoroughly enjoyed reading your latest manuscript, *Wealth: It's In Your Worship Not Your Work*. I read it with studied interest, carefully highlighting key points and making note of particular ideas and concepts that I felt I wanted to revisit and or give more thought and reflection. A treatise of this type is not to be consumed but to be savored morsel by morsel. As you promised, the manuscript was engaging and made easy to read. It was inspiring, enlightening, and instructive. The core concept provided a new and refreshing approach to a fairly well worked subject both in the Christian and Secular markets. The fresh illustrations, stories, and historical bites heightened my interest and helped to validate for me some of the new ideas or points that I was hearing for the first time. I liked your outline which carefully laid down the biblical foundation before developing the practical applications which you begin to cover in the final chapter. I applaud you on the Memory Cards which I think were a nostalgic carry-over from early Primary and Junior Sabbath School days. They worked like linchpins which provided excellent transition (changing points) to the next chapter. They kept me, as the reader, in a state of anticipation much like the "Trailers" that movie theaters uses before a featured film. *Wealth: It's In Your Worship Not Your Works* will be well-received by the wide reader audience you have developed and will launch an entire new fan base as a premier for new readers and students of Christian Stewardship and Resource Development."

- Alvin M. Kibble,
Vice-President North American Division of Seventh-day Adventists,
Silver Spring, MD

"You may wonder how wealth and worship go together, but as you read this book, spiritual gems will regularly be added, and you will find out the real meaning of value in the truest sense."

- Ivan L. Williams, Sr., D.Min.
Ministerial Director
North American Division of Seventh-day Adventists,
Silver Spring, MD

"Excellent commentary on and integration of four important dimensions of a Christian's life: Sabbath, worship, vocation, and wealth. An important read for anyone struggling with meaning in any of those areas. Use of the 'wise worker bee, Shabbat' parable is masterfully done."

- Lilya Wagner, Ph.D.
Director, Philanthropic Service for Institutions,
Silver Spring, MD

"Dr. Roland Hill's new book, *Wealth: It's In Your Worship Not Your Works*, is an innovative look at an important topic. You'll find the book to be entertaining, challenging, and insightful, but most of all, these concepts will change your life! These biblically based principles are so clearly outlined and so logical, you'll wonder why you haven't heard this before. I highly recommend this book."

- Mike Tucker
Speaker/Director, Faith For Today Television
Host of Lifestyle Magazine and Mad About Marriage,
Simi Valley, CA

"During your journey through this insightful book you will arrive at the original outpost of wealth and worship. With unique twists, Dr. Hill leads the reader into another economy and the significance of wealth creation. You will discover both the simple and profound foundation for functioning within God's economic design. If you want a healthy economy – this book provides critical insight."

- Brett A. Elder
Executive Director Stewardship Council
Executive Editor NIV Stewardship Study Bible,
Grand Rapids, MI

"My good friend, Dr. Roland Hill, has once again used his brilliant mind and deeply rooted faith in Jesus Christ to provide readers with new insights on the often controversial subject of wealth. He shows us that by being filled with God's ideas, thoughts and words, we have the gift within us to create value, both for ourselves and others. We can be God's change agents, bringing hope and healing to so many who are downtrodden and discouraged. What a privilege to be used by our Creator this way!"

- Kathy Dudley, D.Min.
Director of Cross-Cultural Empowerment
Professor of Leadership and Community Development
Bakke Graduate University, Dallas, TX

"In every generation God chooses a voice that He fills with enlightenment to bring hope, understanding, and courage to the Body of Christ. Dr. Hill is that voice on wealth creation that takes us back to the Sabbath and shows us the true gift of wealth that we have missed. He brings truth in a style that is both uplifting and satisfying as it quenches our spiritual thirst."

- David W. Trusty
Pastor, Upper Room Fellowship,
Columbia, MD

"This book is a refreshing look at worship and its implications for wealth creation. As a multi-faceted professional (pastor, professor, and entrepreneur), I have personally experienced the dangers of becoming distracted with personal wealth creation. It is only in the context of regular worship that one can develop the acumen to understand, implement, and apprehend the wealth that God graciously extends to His children as they visit with Him in worship."

- D. C. Nosakhere Thomas, D.Min.
Senior Pastor, Rainbow Community Praise Center,
Fontana, CA

"In today's hard economic times, Dr. Roland Hill challenges conventional wisdom by taking on the issue of wealth creation and making sure that it finds its true meaning in the Sabbath and worship - a very significant approach to the way we relate to wealth. The reader will find Dr. Hill's creative thinking in this book very refreshing."

- Zebron Ncube, D.Min.,
Senior Pastor, Highland Avenue Church,
Benton Harbor, MI

"In this groundbreaking new volume, Dr. Hill has added great value to our understanding of God's intention for giving wealth to His children, and our own understanding of our place and potential as Children of God, created in God's image. He expertly takes to task tacitly accepted beliefs in civil religion which virtually and inappropriately suggest that Jesus was a capitalist. It is a provocative, pastoral contribution to both the church and the academy. This book is a necessary addition to the libraries of conscientious pastors, students, and laypeople who are interested in real transformative biblical stewardship."

- Peter Wherry, D.Min.,
Senior Pastor, Mayfield Memorial Missionary Baptist Church, Charlotte, NC

"Dr. Hill dares us to believe that the invisible economy of God is more real than the visible economy of man. If we honor the Life Rhythm, the Giver of every good and perfect gift will supply us with more than just tangible riches from His heavenly bank."

- David Long,
Director of Stewardshsip, Southern Union Conference of Seventh-day Adventists, Decatur, GA

"This book exposes a key conflict in the mind of man and a most important difference between the thinking of God and the thinking of man. If we as humans could reorient our minds according to the blueprint laid out in this book, our lives would be significantly happier, more successful, and our worship to and with God would be more rewarding."

- Robert W. Wernick,
*Retired Comptroller, Cobalt International Energy,
Ottawa, TN*

"Worship is the byword of the true follower of Christ. Dr. Roland Hill effectively articulates the correlation and significance of the Bible Sabbath with God's gift of wealth. His consistent spiritual insight into Scriptural values ties together in this volume theology and Christian practices in a profoundly unique way. This work is worthy of your acquisition for spiritual development and biblical understanding on the subject of God's view of wealth and worship."

- Samuel Thomas, Jr.
Periodical Marketing Director Review and Herald Publishing Association, Hagerstown, MD

"If anyone has any doubts about their self-worth or value, this book is a must read. God has truly manifested Himself in the pages of this book with Kingdom principles and concepts about how one can be truly wealthy through a proper worship connection. The concepts are not only clear but also refreshing, reassuring, and restoring, especially in a world where doubt, fear, and confusion seek to constantly manipulate the mind."

- Charles Sanders,
Stewardship Director, Southwest Regional Conference of Seventh-day Adventists, Dallas, TX

WHAT LEADERS ARE SAYING

"This book is fresh revelation; wealth and worship redefined. Wealth is a gift. Worship reveals and releases the gift. Sabbath rest is optimization technology for a world full of people spinning out of control chasing the wind of worship-less wealth. Read this book and reset for true wealth. Thank you big brother for yet another quantum leap in my understanding of God's love."

- Hallerin Hilton Hill
Radio Talk Show Host,
Knoxville, TN

"In worldwide economic uncertainty, there is a need for an encouraging, faith-centered proclamation from the Christian community. This is it. Dr. Roland J. Hill (my Dad) boldly provides a theologically sound, practical, upbeat economic forecast. From the opening bell, the book grabs you and lays out a comprehensive, fresh look at stewardship."

- Mian R. Hill
Hospital Chaplain, Morton Plant Hospital,
Clearwater, FL

WHY THIS BOOK?

This is a motivational book. I wrote this book for the primary purpose of inspiring the reader with the ideas that have kept me excited, productive, and passionate all of my professional life. Like you, I have experienced the ups and downs, the bad and the good, the failures and successes, but it has been this understanding of wealth that has kept me balanced, buoyant, and blessed. No, I haven't written this book to help you become a millionaire, even though I do know God will entrust the gift of millions to some who read and live out the principles in this book, I've written this book to inspire you. My major concern throughout this book is to help you, the reader, see yourself as God sees you: valuable, worthy, and thus wealthy. My heart bleeds as I watch the masses of people caught in the pursuit of material wealth at the expense of their worship of God, only to be disappointed either by never getting material wealth or by the emptiness they discover once they obtain it.

I really do believe wealth is a gift. Once I unearthed this wealth concept in the Sabbath mine, I was free to live my life unchained by the illusive pursuit of material wealth. Honestly, coming to this understanding hasn't been easy, because I, too, have had to fight against ideologies that war against this God philosophy. I struggle, like you, to keep balanced in a world that tells me that I'm worth something only if I have something, a world that pushes me to believe my self-worth is tied to my net worth, and that views me as something of worth based on my pedigree, posterity, and pigmentation. But it has been the Sabbath truth that confirmed in me who I am, whose I am, and what I am truly worth. The weekly pilgrimage to worship God has been my wellspring. It has been my water at the bottom of the financial barrel, my well in my financial deserts, my reality check in my financial success. What I am sharing with you in this book is from my heart, gleaned from more than five decades of walking with God and nearly forty years of ministry. The information discovered in this book is grounded in the infallible wisdom of the ages, the Bible and illustrated by three original fables that I have written about *Shabbat, The Worker Bee*, to rivet the concepts in your mind. Personally speaking, after reading dozens of wealth creation books and economics textbooks, I found the Bible to be the best economics textbook ever written, outlining the soundest principles on wealth creation. I believe there is a triple blessing (spiritual, social, and financial) awaiting you as you read this book. Be blessed.

- Dr. Roland J. Hill

INTRODUCTION

For nearly forty years, I have worked through, meditated on, researched, and studied biblical concepts of wealth in my search for the truth about wealth. It has been a difficult journey through the jungle of wealth misinformation that exist outside of the Bible. The truth about wealth is tangled up, tied up, and hidden in the undergrowth of non-biblical philosophies many of which are unsuitable for Christian consumption. This book is the clearing in the jungle. I have chopped away much of the undergrowth so that you can see and experience the true meaning of wealth. You will discover that wealth is a gift. It is not something you earn, but something you receive. Only after hacking through the thick jungle of wealth misinformation with my biblical machete (large cutting tool used in the jungle) did I come to understand this revolutionary concept about wealth as a gift. Ironically, for many years, even as a Sabbath observer, I was lost in the jungle of misinformation about wealth. I read good books on wealth creation, but I never discovered the Mother lode. I kept cutting away the thick choking vines of the Puritan work ethic, the boot-strapping philosophy, and the prosperity gospel, searching for wealth's true meaning. I felt, at times, like Indiana Jones in the movie *Raiders of the Lost Ark*, as I chopped down long-standing trees of religious tradition and overgrown shrubs of New Age philosophy in search of the Mother Lode. When I finally cut-a-way a clearing in the jungle of wealth misinformation, I realized that the Mother Lode, the big vein, had been right in front of me all the time. The Mother Lode is the Sabbath. It is the principal vein to the understanding and receiving of wealth. As I dug into the Mother Lode of the Sabbath, the riches in this ancient mine were like striking gold in the Sierra Nevada Mountains in the 1800's. Every shovel scooped up contained wealth beyond my wildest imagination. I no longer felt poor and worthless. Standing in this ancient mine, I knew then that God made humans wealthy. I knew that while wealth may include material possessions ultimately, wealth is about value–God's value of humans and what human's value is in the world. In searching out the meaning of wealth as found in the Sabbath, I discovered Ore Wealth placed in us by God. I found the creative wealth genius that is in every person and recognized why a weekly pilgrimage to the ancient mine to worship God is essential. This is no ordinary book. This book will open to you deep treasures that will completely change your outlook on wealth and yourself. You will leave this book cheerfully obeying the Law of Dependence as the Divine Law of Attraction is activated in your life. This book will open to you the abundant life discovered through a biblical understanding of the meaning of true wealth and the divine process for creating material wealth.

- Dr. Roland J. Hill

Memory Card

"In the depth of the Sabbath, this eternal mine, one finds God's grace. Grace is God's unmerited favor. It is His unearned generosity bestowed on all of His creation. This eternal attribute of God hidden in the depth of the Sabbath is the essence of the meaning of wealth."

- Dr. Roland J. Hill

CHAPTER ONE
The Mother Lode

It was initially kept a secret. The government of Transvaal, formerly an independent state settled by the Boers, put out a gag order after J. H. Davis, an Englishman, sold the Transvaal Treasury 600 pounds of gold that was discovered near Krudgerdorp on the Witswatersrand reef. To keep the discovery of gold a secret, they ordered Davis out of the country. That was in 1852. But a year later, Jacob Marais, a South African, discovered gold on the banks of the Jukskei River. He too was ordered to keep his mouth shut. No one was to know about the gold, for history had recorded that gold had always caused a big stir with often uncontrollable results. But one Sunday in March of 1886, George Harrison, an Austrian gold miner, stumbled onto the Mother lode. He declared his claim with the then-government of the Zuid Afrikaanse Republiek (ZAR), but sold his claim for a measly 10 pounds because of pressure from the government and his own failure to see the significance of the find. Harrison had discovered the Witswatersrand main reef, the Mother Lode. The secret could no longer be kept and the Witswatersrand Gold Rush ultimately resulting in the establishment of Johannesburg and the gold mine that has produced 40 percent of the world's gold in the last 100 years. As significant as the Witwatersrand main reef is to the gold industry, I have discovered a gold mine of far greater significance–a Mother lode of unlimited wealth. It's been kept a secret. In fact, there has been a gag order put out about it.

The devil doesn't want the world to know about this gold mine. He has ordered those who know about it to keep quiet and others of us, like George Harrison, to underestimate its value. Many have spent years digging in the mine but have missed the wealth vein. Eureka, I have found it! Now you can find it.

Mother lode refers to a principal vein or zone of veins of gold or silver ore. When a Mother lode of gold or silver is discovered, an almost unlimited amount of potential material wealth is made available. In this book you will discover the Mother Lode of true wealth; it is the Sabbath. It is the mine of God where we excavate the ore of truth about wealth from the mind of God. With excitement and expectation our first parents watched the opening of the mine and the uncovering of the Mother Lode on the seventh day of creation week (see Genesis 2:1-3). Rabbi Abraham Heschell wrote, "…the seventh day is a mine where {S}pirit's precious metal can be found…"[1] God took it upon Himself to invite Adam and Eve into the secrets of creation. He called them into Sabbath worship as a time of divine revelation. It was a day of disclosure about who and what God values. It was the beginning of God's instruction on the meaning of true wealth. Amasa Walker, the eighteenth century economist, in his search for a definition of wealth, came to the conclusion that wealth is simply the allocation of value.[2] And at the beginning of creation God created the Mother Lode so that men could have a perpetual place to search out what He values most.

CHAPTER ONE *The Mother Lode*

The Gift Of Wealth

In the depth of the Sabbath, this eternal mine, one finds God's grace. Grace is God's unmerited favor. It is His unearned generosity bestowed on all His creation. This eternal attribute of God hidden in the depth of the Sabbath is the essence of the meaning of wealth. Adam and Eve standing in midst of wealth at the dawn of the history were taught that wealth is a gift from God. Wealth is an unearned favor, a gift, an act of God's grace.

"In the beginning God created the heavens and the earth" (Genesis 1:1). God didn't need to create the earth. He had and has unnumbered angels that show forth His creative power and His unlimited love. Neither was there pressure to create. Out of love God purposed the creation of the world. By grace He called it into existence. Neither nature nor man contributed to creation; it was the sole work of God. Creation is a gift of God's unearned generosity, His grace, and a declaration of His value system. Simply put, wealth is a gift of grace.

This was a fresh revelation for me, both in terms of grace and a new understanding of wealth. As a theologian and a pastor, I have always defined and described grace in the context of sin. Grace has always been thought of as an acquired attribute of God, an attribute that developed after sin. But rediscovering that grace is an eternal attribute, helped me to understsand that grace predates sin because it is an inherent attribute of God. And wealth, it has always been viewed as a by-product of work and definitely not a gift. Wealth was never seen as God's value but human's production.

"The heavens declare the glory of God, and the sky above proclaims his handiwork. Day to day pours out speech and night to night reveals knowledge" (Psalm 19: 1-2). In the intricate details of creation, God's value system is seen. In the elegant design of nature, He shows forth the worth He assigns to animate and inanimate objects. "And God saw that it was good" (Genesis 1: 10). These words announced God's thoughts about His world. God values His creation. But that value is only in relationship to God and man. The creation in and of itself has no value. It has value because God gives it value. In the Sabbath mine, God taught Adam and Eve the worth of His creation, thus shaping their understanding of wealth as provided by Him. Our first parents learned that the value of animate and inanimate objects was determined, not by their existence, but by the assessment placed on it first by God, then by man.

Man's Value

Ellen G. White, a nineteenth century prolific writer and American Christian pioneer states, "Upon all created things is seen the impress of the Deity. Nature testifies of God. The susceptible mind, brought in contact with the miracle and mystery of the universe, cannot but recognize the working of infinite power. Not by its own inherent energy does the earth produce its bounties, and year by year continue its motion around the sun. An unseen hand guides the planets in their circuit of the heavens. A mysterious life pervades all nature –a life that sustains the unnumbered worlds throughout immensity, that lives in the insect atom which floats in the summer breeze, that wings the flight of the swallow and feeds the young ravens which cry, that brings the bud to blossom and the flower to fruit."[3] As valuable as the world is, its value is subordinate to man's value. The earth was made for man, not man for the earth. God's inaugural speech to our first parents was a statement of value. "So God created man in His own image, in the image of God he created him; male and female he created them" (Genesis 1:28). Animate and inanimate objects were spoken into existence; man on the other hand came from the hand of God (Genesis 2:7). Man's value is determined from the order used for creating him and appraised by the method of making him; God the Model, God the Maker. God's value statement is unmistakably clear: "You are valuable. You were created in My image. You were created to be like Me." Can we think less of ourselves than God thinks about us? God's inaugural speech continued, "Rule over the fish and the birds of the air and over every living creature that moves on the ground" (see Genesis 1:28). This was God's positional statement, "You were given dominion, rulership over creation." This godlike quality, was only given to man. In God's final inaugural statement, He was proclaiming: "You are of higher value than the material world. You don't derive your value from created things, but Me."

Digging deep in the Sabbath mine you come to understand, as I have, that God is the source of all value and that there is no value without God. In a real sense then, God alone assigns value, He is the quintessence of all wealth. Therefore in God, not in the created world, we find worth, the essence of true wealth. Evidenced in the order of the creation and His personal involment in the creation of man is God's statement of value for the human family. God created the world, then man—not man, then the world.

Standing in the entrance of the Sabbath mine, God had our first parents ponder this fact that wealth was not based on man's work but on God's grace. Adam and Eve's first full day of life was a rest day–not a workday. It was a day of worship-not a day of work. Wealth was a gift from God. The order of true wealth creation, as stated by God's resting on the Sabbath, is always worship first–then wealth creation. "Seek first the kingdom of God and his righteousness and all these things will be added to you" (Matthew 6:33).

Wealth from God's perspective was never about the accumulation of material possessions. In its truest sense, wealth is and always has been about value that comes out of relationship. "You shall remember the Lord your God, for it is he who gives you the power to get wealth, that he may establish his covenant which He swore to your fathers, as it is this day" (Deuteronomy 8:18). God stated his covenant relationship with Adam and Eve by creating them with wealth and confirmed it with Israel by giving them the power to produce wealth. True wealth is a sign of the covenant between God and man.

From Riches to Rags

Our first parents were not a "Horatio Alger story." They did not go from "rags to riches" but from "riches to rags." Adam and Eve were born wealthy. They were created in wealth, with wealth, and with the power to produce wealth. Locked inside the mind of the original pair was Ore Wealth placed there by God. From this original ore, discovered in the Sabbath mine by Adam and Eve, all physical wealth would be created.

"Out of the ground the Lord God had formed every beast of the field and every bird of the heavens and brought them to the man to see what he would call them. And whatever the man called every living creature, that was its name" (Genesis 2:19). This was man's first act of creating wealth. God now provided him with the opportunity to exercise this dominion responsibility in a way that established his authority and supremacy—in ancient times, it was an act of authority to impose names (cf. Daniel 1:7) and an act of submission to receive them. God-given ideas for the naming of the birds and animals was an act of placing value. God showed His value of man by giving him the privilege of naming (giving value to animals and birds). We all understand that when you name something, you are superior or of more value than the thing named. In all of mankind is Ore Wealth. God has given us the gift of creating value, naming the creation, therefore creating wealth. "As it is written, 'I have made you the father of many nations'–in the presence of the God in whom he believed, who gives life to the dead and calls into existence the things that do not exist" (Romans 4:17).

True Worship

There is a seismic struggle to find value and self-worth among twenty-first century man. And what I have observed is that the struggle over self-worth and value is really a struggle about worship. True worship is in serious decline. In its place we have put work or pleasure. Twenty-first century man believes he must earn his worth. He believes that worth is in what he possesses. Therefore, ceasing from work, which is the requirement of true worship, decreases, he believes, the ability to earn wealth, thus affecting one's self-worth. Modern people no longer see the need of retreating to the Sabbath Mine to worship God. Worship and work are not seen as analogous terms. Therefore, worship is neglected, which results in the loss of self-worth, value, and a clear direction in life. Sabbath rest was designed by God to replenish value given out over six days of work. We do not have an unlimited source of value, only God. Therefore, God must constantly replenish us.

What is worship? Worship is recognizing the awesomeness of God. It is confessing our creatureliness before God. It is accepting His ownership of all things. It is acknowledging Him as the source of all value. Worship is thanking God for His gift of wealth to man. True worship replenishes worth and value because in worship God breathes value anew into us. He reminds us of His gift of dominion and the ability to create value by naming the world around us. He confirms to us, "We are because He is – therefore, we have because He is." Only in worship does that revelation come. Worship is where we receive the deepest revelation of God and His value of us. Tied up in Sabbath worship is the truth: wealth is a gift from God. Sabbath observance says, "We are because He is – therefore, we have because He is." Wealth is in your worship not your works.

Memory Card

"Wealth is a gift, and those who have discovered the secret, work less and worship more. They have discovered, by experience and observation, that unending work, as the means for creating wealth, is a myth. Work in and of itself has no power to create wealth. It can produce energy, activity, and even create an illusion of wealth, but it can never create wealth."

- Dr. Roland J. Hill

CHAPTER TWO
The Secret

It was at the end of the first six-day work-week that God completed His initial creative work. One breath, in a nanosecond, would have been sufficient to create the planet, but instead, God deliberately sectioned off eternity: morning and evening; day and night; days–seven days, to be exact. God created, what I call, a life rhythm for His new creation called time. Time would be the boundary for work, worship, leisure, rest, and ultimately, wealth creation for His new creature. It is our reminder that only God is timeless. While created in the image of an eternal God, we are not eternal. We are created beings, not creators. Time becomes man's reminder, regulator, and equalizer.

Wealth creation ideas in the twenty-first century collide with time–the life rhythm. Time is often viewed by modern man as an antagonist to wealth creation. You hear the vilification of time in expressions like: 'If I had only more time;" "If only there were more hours in a day;" "If I had more days in the week;" and "If I had an extra day." These expressions are reflective of a desire to be released from the boundaries or limits of time. A more literal translation of these expressions is, "I would be happier and more prosperous if I didn't have time restrictions." Living life outside of the life rhythm as modern man suggests, is reminiscent of the fable *Shabbat and The Secret*.

Shabbat and the Secret

There was a wise worker bee named Shabbat who lived far away in a thriving beehive. But unlike the other worker bees, Shabbat was known for her unusual work schedule, for long life, and for a high output of honey.

"Shabbat, why are you always so energetic and happy?" chirped Lunae.

"It's the secret!" whispered Shabbat, as she flew off to gather her assigned portion of nectar for the day. Lunae stood pondering what Shabbat had just said as she, too, went back to work. That evening while the beehive was still buzzing, Lunae noticed that Shabbat had turned in for the night.

"Lunae, look at Shabbat. All of us are busy working and she's over there sleeping!" Solis retorted. "I'm going to check her production chart."

To Solis' surprise, Shabbat had not only made her daily quota, but surpassed it by ten percent. Solis gathered several of her close friends together to discuss this mystery. There was Mercuri, the highest producer in the hive; Iovis–the hardest worker; Veneris–the deepest thinker; Lunae–the most analytical; and Marti– the most fearless.

CHAPTER TWO *The Secret*

Gathering around the bottom board of the hive, Solis spoke, "How can this be? How can Shabbat produce so much more that all of us?"

"She must have help. I've calculated your findings of Shabbat's production and the only answer is additional help," Mercuri spoke with authority.

"But, who in the hive has time to help? Everyone is barely able to keep up with their own quota," Veneris thoughtfully chimed in. After several rounds of probing questions, the group went off to bed without answers.

"Good morning everyone. Time to start the day!" Shabbat bugled, buzzing with joy as she fluttered around the hive prepared to start a day of gathering pollen.

"Shabbat, how do you produce so much honey with fewer hours of work than us?" Lunae quizzed Shabbat again.

"It's the secret." Shabbat smiled and then quickly disappeared, leaving Lunae in deep thought. Every day Shabbat worked from sunup to sundown, but when the sun set her work stopped.

In spite of Shabbat's production, she was called into the hive office and questioned about her hours of work.

"Shabbat, I've studied your time card.

You only work 40 hours a week and don't work at all on Saturday. I am getting complaints from the other bees about your work ethic," shouted Victoria, the big boss.

"Miss Victoria, can I ask a question?" Shabbat meekly responded.

"Go ahead," retorted Victoria.

"Miss, have you examined my production rate?"

"Yes, and that's the problem. No one can understand how you can produce so much with so few hours," Victoria shouted. "Can you explain this mystery?" Victoria asked.

"Miss, it's the secret." Shabbat was calm and resolute as she spoke.

"Secret or not, you must immediately begin working like the other bees or your job is at stake. Out of here now, and get to work!" Victoria terminated the conversation and had Shabbat escorted out of the hive office.

The entire beehive began to buzz about Shabbat's office encounter and wondered what her response would be the next day.

"Good morning everyone. Time to start the day!" Shabbat bugled, buzzing with joy as she fluttered around the hive, prepared to start a new day of gathering pollen as if nothing had happened. That evening Shabbat folded her wings and quietly went off to bed, just as she had

CHAPTER TWO *The Secret*

always done, while all the other bees continued their work. As the days wore into weeks, Solis gathered Mercuri, Iovis, Veneris, Lunae, and Marti.

"Ladies, how are you feeling?" Tiredness was in Solis' voice as she pushed out the words.

Marti responded first, "I feel like walking death. This unending work is about to kill me."

A unified and mournful sigh burst from the entire group in agreement with Marti's statement.

"But have you notice Shabbat?" Iovis spoke up.

"Yes, she seems as vibrant as her first day on the job." Mercuri whispered.

"How is she doing it?" Veneris voiced the question for the group.

"Good morning everyone. Time to start the day!" Shabbat bugled, buzzing with joy as she fluttered around the hive prepared to start a day of gathering pollen. But on this day the hive was silent, she only heard the faint voices of a few bees. Shabbat flitted toward the sound of the voices. There lay Solis, Mercuri, Iovis, Veneris, Lunae, and Marti. The tired look had now turned to the familiar look of the death ritual that the hive regularly endured. In just a matter of minutes and they would die just like the thousands of others in the beehive.

Solis strained to turn her head as Shabbat entered the cell.

"Sorry, ladies. I really hate to see you in this condition." Shabbat fought back the tears.

"How did you do it?" Solis spoke, gasping for air.

"Do what?" Shabbat responded.

"How have you stayed productive and vibrant, while out-living us?" Veneris snapped.

"It's the secret," Lunae quickly answered for Shabbat. As Lunae closed her eyes in death, she whispered, "I only wish I had asked her the secret." *

The Work Myth

While work is a significant part of wealth creation, it is not the secret. Like the worker bees in the fable, many in the twenty-first century have mistaken unending work as the secret of a productive and prosperous life. Wealth is a gift, and those who have discovered the secret work less and worship more. They have discovered, by experience and observation, that unending work, as the means for creating wealth, is a myth. Work in and of itself has no power to create wealth. It can produce energy, activity, and even create an illusion of wealth, but it can never create lasting wealth.

The myth of wealth creation through hard work in the West has, to a large extent, been fostered by the religious ideology known as the Puritan Work Ethic. The Puritan Work

Ethic is defined as a belief in and devotion to hard work, duty, thrift, self-discipline, and responsibility as a means for creating wealth. This religious philosophy is based on the sixteenth century reformer John Calvin's teaching of double predestination. It emphasizes the necessity of hard work as an expression of one's personal calling and worldly success as a visible sign or result (not a cause) of personal salvation. Work, for those who believe in or have been influenced by Calvin's teaching, takes on a redemptive quality. It is imbued with saving virtue and for many, becomes a form of worship. The more one works, the better person one becomes and the more visible signs of one's hard work, through the accumulation of things, the more evidence of one's personal salvation. But the Puritan Work Ethic has not been so pure. Think about it. For the millions of people who put in long grueling hours on backbreaking jobs, where is the wealth? How has the promise of the Puritan Work Ethic been fulfilled for the millions around the world? And for those who have accumulated material wealth from this philosophy, what has the wealth really done for their quality of life?

Unending work, which is part and parcel of the Puritan Work Ethic, causes one to forget the source of wealth. It creates in man an attitude of self-sufficiency that evolves into the self-made-man syndrome. What I have discovered is that self-made men are convinced that success can be explained by only one word (repeated over and over again) namely work, work, work. In this philosophy there is little room for worship. Man becomes his own source of wealth. Seven-day workweeks are the norm. Worship is viewed as an enemy to wealth creation. Therefore, time is allocated for only one major thing: work.

With the diminishing of worship, self-made man sees his value only in the light of work. Rather than seeing himself as God sees him, wealthy, a self-made man sees himself as a poor man in search of wealth. It's the rags-to-riches story. What sells best in the twenty-first century is the Horatio Alger story, which is based on the idea that a person from a humble background can, over time, move to middle-class security and comfort through hard work, determination, courage, and honesty. While the Horatio Alger story makes great motivational material, the danger of this mythological story is that it steals man's true worth by causing him to break the life rhythm. Work is viewed as the secret of wealth creation, and like the worker bees in the fable, man spends his time and energy at the expense of worship and rest. He falls under the spell of work that sends him in the pursuit of wealth he already has, but just doesn't realize. Wealth is a gift. We were created in wealth, with wealth, and with the power to produce wealth. Wealth isn't what one does, but what one is.

Relationship To Riches

This is expressed best in the Adam and Eve story. Adam and Eve, the original pair, began with wealth. For them, wealth creation began with abundance. Theirs was not the "rags-to-riches" story but the "riches to rags" story. Remember, Adam and Eve's first full day on the planet wasn't a workday but a worship day. This first worship day, Sabbath, laid the foundation for understanding the source of true wealth, God. It introduced the original pair to God's wealth-creation formula. They discovered in the Sabbath mine that God's formula of wealth creation leads to a "relationship-to-riches" story.

Our first parents discovered the secret: Time, the life rhythm. Time calibrates life and is anchored by the Sabbath. Time was designed to foster relationships. Morning and evening give boundaries to daily work (see Genesis1:5); having six days of labor restricts weekly work (see Exodus 20:9); and one day of Sabbath rest (see Deuteronomy 5: 14) prohibits work, all for the express purpose of protecting relationships, first, between God and man and then, between man and man. This life rhythm is the secret to wealth creation because it declares God as the source of all wealth, shows that man's wealth creation has limits, and affirms that wealth is not determined by ones work but by a relationship with God in worship.

Shabbat and the Secret written by Roland J. Hill

Memory Card

"The Law of Dependence states that one must recognize that God is self-existent, eternal, and Creator of everything, and only in adherence to the Law of Dependence can created beings find true security and can created things have value."

- Dr. Roland J. Hill

CHAPTER THREE

The Law of Dependence

Shabbat and the Law of Dependance

*D*eep in the lush green forest of Edora lived a well-known colony of bees. All over the world there was talk of this highly productive beehive. Everyone talked about their unusual honey. It was truly something to talk about. Nowhere in the whole wide world could such honey be found. It was tantalizingly sweet with an iridescent glow that burst forth from its deep golden color. Everyone knew that it was the twelve different wildflowers that held the secret to this remarkable honey. These enchanted flowers grew all over Edora and bloomed year-round, each type of flower in its own separate part of the forest. But while the honey was the centerpiece of conversation, there was an undercurrent of talk about the bees themselves. They were unusual. It seemed that the bees were totally reliant on Queen Beetris, the ruler of the hive. There was a bit of irony. The bees were all self-starters, thinkers, and hard workers, but for an entire 24-hour period, once a week, they hovered around Queen Beetris as if their lives depended on it. The undercurrent of talk was that they were governed by some strange law known as the Law of Dependence. The law wasn't written anywhere, but every bee knew it and lived by it.

On the east side of Edora lay an unnamed barren desert. In this desert lived an unproductive, undisciplined colony of bees. They did produce honey, but only when they wanted to. No one wanted it. It had a slightly rancid smell and a dirty gold color. It was so undesirable that it stayed in the hive cells until it crystallized and fell to the ground as dust. Queen Diva was ruler of this unnamed colony, but everyone knew she didn't rule; she just reproduced. The only law that governed the hive was the law of self-interest. "You are the master of your own fate," was the motto of the hive. "Depend on no one but you," were the words in bold letters scribbled across the dull yellowish and brown-striped tummy of the bees.

Queen Diva, like everyone else, heard about the bees from Edora and their tantalizingly sweet honey. She had to find out their secret.

"Lucky, go to Edora and find out why all the talk about those bees," Queen Diva snapped the order.

"Yes, ma'am," Lucky spoke as she jetted away.

On arrival in Edora, Lucky was startled.

CHAPTER THREE *The Law of Dependance*

She had never seen such beauty. The lush green foliage of Edora was decorated by the twelve types of enchanted flowers that filled the air with twelve different perfumes oozing from each petal. Edora was truly a paradise. It was a stark contrast to the barren desert and puny flowers Lucky only knew. As she approached the hive, Lucky observed the orderliness of the colony, but what caught her attention was the honey. Honey like she had never seen. There it was, tantalizingly sweet with an iridescent glow that burst forth from its deep golden color.

"Hello, you're new here. Can I help you?" Shabbat greeted Lucky with her energetic smile and warm words.

"Yes, I've been sent to find out why the world is talking about your colony," Lucky spoke guardedly.

"I'll be glad to show you around and answer your questions," Shabbat chirped. "Let me first introduce you to our leader," Shabbat continued.

"Queen Beetris, this is Lucky. She's here to find out why there's so much talk about us," Shabbat smiled as she finished her introduction.

"Welcome, young lady. There's not much to find out, but you are welcome to look around and we will answer your questions as best we can," Queen Beetris spoke nonchalantly.

With that, Shabbat escorted Lucky off on a tour of the hive. Lucky observed the teams of bees being dispatched to different parts of the forest bringing back nectar from the twelve different enchanted flowers.

"Ah, that's what everyone's talking about," Lucky said to herself. "The secret is in the flowers." All week long Lucky watched the bees diligently gathering and storing the precious nectar from the enchanted flowers.

"This is a different bunch of bees," Lucky muttered. She noticed that all the bees kept checking in with Queen Beetris. It was as if they wouldn't do anything without her approval.

"Shabbat, can't you all think for yourself?" Lucky finally blurted out.

Shabbat smiled and replied, "Why, yes, we can, and yes, we do. Why do you ask?"

"It seems that you all are totally dependent on Queen Beetris. What's the deal?"

Shabbat turned her head with an admiring gaze in the direction of Queen Beetris and then timidly spoke, "Just keep watching. You'll understand." It was at the end of the week when Lucky noticed that the entire hive stopped working. Not one bee left the hive. Not one bee flew off to gather nectar from the enchanted flowers.

Startled, Lucky spoke up, "What's going on?"

"We're simply obeying the Law of Dependence." Shabbat cheerfully chirped.

"What is the Law of Dependence?" Lucky's curiously asked.

"It's kind of hard to explain," Shabbat responded, "but I'll give it a try."

"The beehive recognizes that without Queen Beetris, the colony is nothing. Once a week we stop, as evidence of our dependence on her."

"Don't you get tired of this once-a-weekly ritual?" Lucky bellowed.

Shabbat smiled, "Only those who don't know who they are get tired." She continued,

"It's dependence that keeps us alive and productive. We all know that dependence on Queen Beetris is our survival and security."

Lucky shook her head with disappointment and mused as she began her journey back to the unnamed hive. "So that's what the world is talking about." she said. "Total dependence; that's too risky," Lucy pondered as she disappeared.*

The Pursuit of Wealth

Security serves as the hot button for the pursuit of wealth. Many grab hold of the belief that in an unsecure, uncertain, and shaky world, material wealth will provide security. Fear for the future causes many to stockpile material wealth through CDs, IRAs, stocks, bonds, cash, gold, silver, and property in an attempt to ward off fear. Ironically, the more material wealth accumulated, the less secure one feels. Thus begins an endless pursuit of wealth in the search of safety and security through the accumulation of more and more.

The pursuit of wealth boils down to dependence. The ultimate question is, "What or who will we depend on?" Stepping back into the Sabbath mine again, we discover an unusual law—The Law of Dependence. This law states that God is self-existent, eternal, and Creator of everything, and only in adherence to the Law of Dependence can created beings find true security and can created things have value.

The Meaning of Manna

God in the wilderness illustrated this Law of Dependence shortly after Israel was delivered from Egypt. In the Sinai desert, Israel feared death by starvation. "And the whole congregation of the people of Israel grumbled against Moses and Aaron in the wilderness, and the people said to them, 'Would that we had died by the hand of the Lord in the land of Egypt, when we sat by the meat pots and ate bread to the full. For you have brought us into this wilderness to kill this whole assembly with hunger'" (Exodus 16:2- 3). God's response was first, ... to satisfy their tangible need for security and then, to teach them about true security. He sent quail in the evening and the morning of the next day, heavenly flakes. These unknown flakes from heaven drew this response from the Israelites, "When

CHAPTER THREE *The Law of Dependance*

the people of Israel saw it, they said to one another, 'What is this?' (Exodus 16:15). This unrecognized food stork was called Manna. The giving of Manna became Israel's instructions on the Law of Dependence. In simple terms, from my interpretation, God informed them, "I have heavenly provisions to provide for My creatures even in impossible situations. You can depend on Me." In His instructions for gathering the Manna, God emphasized dependence. The requirement was to gather just what they could eat for one day, one omer (an ancient unit of measure). Nothing was to be held over for the next day. "And he humbled you and let you hunger and fed you with Manna, which you did not know, nor did your fathers know, that He might make you to know that man does not live by bread alone, but man lives by every word that comes from the mouth of the Lord" (Deuteronomy 8:3). God's daily declaration in the gathering of the Manna was, "Your security is in Me, your Sovereign Lord, not your surplus." The proclamation was driven home when those who feared for tomorrow held over Manna until the next day. "But they did not listen to Moses. Some left part of it till the morning, and it bred worms and stank" (Exodus 16:20). Hoarded wealth, surplus held back for security, will not provide security. It can only provide a false sense of safety that, in the end, ruins its owner.

God led Israel back to the Sabbath mine to further teach the Law of Dependence. "On the sixth day they gathered twice as much bread, two omers each. And when all the leaders of the congregation came to Moses, he said to them, 'This is what the Lord has commanded: 'Tomorrow is a day of solemn rest, a holy Sabbath to the LORD; bake what you will bake and boil what you will boil, and all that is left over lay aside to be kept till the morning.' So they laid it aside till the morning, as Moses commanded them, and it did not stink, and there were no worms in it. Moses said, 'Eat it today, for today is a Sabbath to the LORD; today you will not find it in the field. Six days you shall gather it, but on the seventh day, which is the Sabbath, there will be none" (Exodus 16:22-26). Emphatically, God gave assurance to the fearful recently freed slaves, "I have heavenly provisions to provide for My creatures even in impossible situations. You can depend on Me."

The instructions for gathering the Manna contained the promise of provision and preservation for Israel's survival and security. The Law of Dependence states again that one must recongize that God is self-existent, eternal, and Creator of everything, and only in adherence to the Law of Dependence can created beings find true security and can created things have value. By obeying God's instructions for the gathering and storing of the Manna, Israel adhered to the Law of Dependence and reaped the benefits.

Total Dependence

But candidly speaking, many twenty-first century people struggles with the Law of Dependence. Like Lucky in the fable, total dependence is too risky. Unending work for many twenty-first century people is a prerequisite for wealth, and wealth is their security. The questions arise: If I stop working for an entire day, who will take up the slack? Is God really that dependable? Again, the pursuit of wealth boils down to what

CHAPTER THREE *The Law of Dependance*   57

or whom we will depend on. In the giving of the Manna, God demonstrated to Israel that they could depend on Him. Total dependence on God is a major indicator of our belief about God. By our dependence on God we show what do we really believe about God.

These are the essential questions: Do we believe God is self-existent, eternal, and creator? Do we believe that He created us? The answer to these questions show whether or not we are totally depending on God. In the fable, Shabbat, the worker bee expressed it well, "Only those who don't know who they are get tired. It's dependence that keeps us alive and productive. We all know that dependence on Queen Beetris is our survival and security."

The Story of Eugene Roddy

Eugene Roddy, a retired farmer, shares his story of obedying the Law of Dependence. "I grew up on a farm and was a farmer myself for 40 years. Early in life I was taught Bible principles, particularly Sabbath observance and tithing. No matter whether the weather was too wet or too dry, too hot or too cold, for the work to be done as originally planned, we never felt the need to plow, plant, or harvest on Sabbath. This principle stayed with me throughout my entire life.

Of course, as a farmer, I was never sure how much, if any, profit I'd realize at the end of a season. So I always figured my tithe and taxes after the crops were harvested and sold. Paying for land and equipment many times required all the income received. In farming operation it is common to have taxable and titheable "income" with no actual cash to pay it. When that happened, as it often did, I'd have to go to a lending institution and borrow money for these items. I didn't like that.

One year, partway through the harvest, I looked at the remaining crops to harvested and estimated I would be approximately $5,000 short of the funds needed to take care of my obligations for land and equipment. But I decied to go ahead and return a tithe of $500 of the crop money I had already received. This would be easier than trying to convince a lending institution to loan me money to give to the church.

To my surprise, when the last portion of the crops was harvested and sold, I received approximately $5,000 more than I had estimated–just the amount I had returned tithe on. After that experience I revised my plan of returning tithe. I gave it on a project income, before I had no cash left, and I have been blessed ever since."[4]

Work Required

But let's be clear, the Law of Dependence does not preclude work. While the Manna was a gift, it was not obtained without effort. God provided bread from heaven, but Israel was required to gather it. Trusting and depending on God in no way negates human effort. Human effort is proof of our belief. Wealth is the allocation of value and our human efforts are proof of what we value. We will only gather, buy, purchase, and sacrifice for what we value. So the real question in the search for security is, "What do we value?" We will only value that which we believe will give us security. The word Manna

CHAPTER THREE *The Law of Dependance*

means, "What is this?" Israel took a minute to decide whether Manna was valuable. They thought about their stomachs and decided Manna had value, then grabbed their bags and filled them with what they valued.

There are those that see the Law of Dependence as an excuse for indolence. They reason, "Since wealth is a gift and I'm depending of God, then there is no need to work." God's unambiguous instructions for the gathering of Manna overturned such reasoning, "This what the LORD commanded: 'Gather of it, each one of you, as much as he can eat" (Exodus 16:16). Just like God doesn't put food in the sparrow's mouth, He didn't put manna in the mouths of the Israelites. Israel, like farmer Eugene Roddy, had to exercise their belief and dependence on God by working, and working daily.

Interestingly enough, the life rhythm came to bear in this teaching of the Law of Dependence. God gave specific times for Israel to gather and not gather the Manna. There was not a random raining down of Manna from Heaven. Manna only fell in the morning and Israel was required to gather it just after dawn in the early hours of that day. Here God reemphasized the life rhythm. Israel wasn't allowed to set their time for gathering Manna, God set the time; Israel must obey. They were not permitted to gather Manna when they thought best. God sets the life rhythm and those who live in the rhythm experience success and security. Those who violate the life rhythm pay a heavy price.

The Law of Dependence not only required work but also, early rising. The quietness of the early hours, undisturbed by daily activities and others, become an excellent time to hear

God's voice clearly and distinctly. There is some truth in the old saying, "The early bird gets the worm." In the early moments of the morning, "the early riser gets the Word." Those who understand the Law of Dependence know that God sustains us by His Word. From His Word all wealth is created. His Word is the currency of His economy. So early in the morning, when there are few distractions, God opens the Bank of Heaven and dispenses to us His ideas, plans, and strategies. These are the building blocks for true wealth creation. Notice again in the giving of the Manna, the life rhythm is honored. Israel gathered Manna six days, but was forbidden by God from gathering on the Sabbath. God's command to "Remember the Sabbath" emphasizes the fact that it is easy to forget the source of wealth as we gather six days a week, therefore He established the prohibition about Sabbath work. It was and is God's way of saying; "Wealth is not in your work, but in your worship."

Memory Card

"All human systems, like the Egyptian economy, are based on existing matter; thus only what you can see is believed to be available for wealth creation. Sight-based economies leave its citizens, as it did Israel, in fear, frustration, and in an illusive pursuit of material wealth."

— Dr. Roland J. Hill

CHAPTER FOUR
The Bank of Heaven

It hit me like a bolt of lighting as I sat at the red light behind the Brinks armored truck. Valueless paper currency was being transported in an armored truck. Paper money, printed data transfers of money, checks, coins, and maybe even a few gold bars all being transported in a bullet-proof truck, spoke straight to heart of the confusion over wealth. Wealth is the assignment and allocation of value. Sitting at the light behind a white mobile fortress, seeing the name "Brinks" printed in bright blue block letters on both sides, was unmistakable proof of where we in the West have assigned and allocated our values. It's in paper, digital transfers, coins, property, and precious materials. It was a reality check for me. Those things have no value in and of themselves; we give them value. But paradoxically, that which we have given value, we now need to give us value. We value it to the point of carrying it around in robber-resistant vehicles, willing to take the life of the very beings that gave it value. Strange, but that's the reality we face in an age when people live by sight and not by faith, who are taught to see only the kingdoms of men, unaware of the Kingdom of God. Christ's message was simple, "Repent, for the kingdom of heaven is at hand" (Matthew 4:17). The Kingdom of Heaven was not a metaphor–it was and is the literal Kingdom of God. Jesus attempted, in His straightforward message, to open the eyes of his followers to Kingdom concepts.

Earth–The Kingdom Outpost

Earth is an outpost of God's eternal Kingdom. At the end of the six-day creation week, God ceased His work to officially inaugurate His new Kingdom outpost. Sabbath, was the inaugural day. On that day, God identified Himself as King, and Adam and Eve as His subjects. The constitution of this new Kingdom outpost was the character of the King, later written as the Ten Commandments. Those same Ten Laws were also the covenant between the King and His subjects and the condition for their prosperity. "And He declared to you his covenant, which He commanded you to perform, that is the Ten Commandments." "You shall remember the LORD your God, for it is He who gives you power to get wealth, that He may confirm His covenant that He swore to your fathers, as it is this day" (Deuteronomy 4:13; 8:18). God introduced Himself as the foundation of the economy of this new outpost and His word as its currency. There would never be a question about the stability of this Kingdom outpost because its economy was based solidly on God Himself.

But studying the history of Israel, we discover that slavery brought Israel to the place where they no longer believed in earth as God's outpost. Their failure to obey God's commands while under oppression closed their eyes to the Kingdom concepts.

The Wilderness Classroom

Ellen G. White, an American Religious leader, who has had an enormous impact on the world's economy through her

CHAPTER FOUR *The Bank of Heaven*

leading edge concepts in health wrote, "In their bondage, the Israelites had to some extent lost the knowledge of God's law, and they had departed from its precepts. The Sabbath had been generally disregarded, and the exactions of their taskmasters made its observance apparently impossible. But Moses had shown his people that obedience to God was the first condition of deliverance; and the efforts made to restore the observance of the Sabbath had come to the notice of their oppressors."[5]

The philosophies of Pharaoh had molded the thinking of Israel and the economy of Egypt had shaped their lives. They went into Egypt as free men and because of their disobedience, emerged as slaves. God's gracious act of delivering Israel from Egypt and leading them into the wilderness was primarily to re-introduce them to His Kingdom and His economy. In the wilderness, Israel had to learn anew the Law of Dependence. Through the daily provision of Manna from His invisible unlimited resources, God proved Himself as their daily bread, "that He might make you to know that man does not live by bread alone, but man lives by every word that comes from the mouth of the Lord" (Deuteronomy 8:3). Centuries later Jesus revealed Himself as the Bread of Life, a corroboration with the miraculous provisions in the wilderness (John 6:32-35). Israel had to learn in the desert, the crucial lesson about the sufficiency of God. The wilderness classroom was the place God chose to re-introduce His Kingdom and His economy.

In the quietness of the desert, away from all human influences, the Israelites were captive students. They had learned to trust in Pharaoh's economy. The skills and trades given by God had been reshaped by the skills and the schemes of a worldly economy. Work was now their god and they had become beholden to Pharaoh's kingdom and limited by a man-made economy. The Israelites were not just oppressed, they became blinded to their real potential. Living out of sync of the life rhythm, Israel learned to live by sight. Survival and success were determined by what they could see, not by what God said. All human systems, like the Egyptian economy, are based on existing matter; thus only what you can see is believed to be available for wealth creation. Sight-based economies leave its citizens, as it did Israel, in fear, frustration, and in an illusive pursuit of material wealth. In order for Israel to understand God's Kingdom, God had to reveal Himself. He had to give evidence of His Kingdom and instructions on His economy and its currency. In the desert, God would teach them how to access His economy for their spiritual, social, and financial prosperity.

    The barren unproductive countryside was an excellent place to learn again about this invisible God and His invisible economy. In Egypt, Israel resorted to worshiping gods of iron, stone, gold– idol gods, gods that they could see. They had become dependent on visible gods who they thought were powerful but in reality were powerless. In the wilderness, as He did at creation on Sabbath, God would teach Israel the most powerful wealth creation principle in the universe: Wealth is in the mind of God, not in the work of man. Even the word Manna expressed the mystery of God's provisions. "What is this?" was Israel's question as they viewed the heavenly provision. God provided for Israel in a way that was beyond their understanding.

The Wilderness Test

In this modern day God still leads us to and through the wilderness. What is the wilderness? The wilderness is the place of barrenness. It's the place where productivity is problematic. It's the place of apparent impossibility where discouragement easily sets in. It's the place that seems almost God-forsaken. In a practical sense, a wilderness could be the loss of a job, a place of decreasing income and increasing expenses, a place of a debilitating illness that results in the loss of a job. Are you in a wilderness? Or have you just recently come through a wilderness and are wondering, "What did I just come through?" Good News! The wilderness can be a good place, if you will open your eyes to see God's possibilities. Understand that God leads us to the wilderness because it is an excellent place to learn to live by faith, not by sight, a good place to learn how to live out the Law of Dependence. Only in the wilderness is our faith tested. Only in the wilderness, when all human resources are no longer available, do we with look to God alone. I personally have discovered that it is in the wilderness that God, in extraordinary ways, introduces us to His economy and escorts us into a Sabbath rest.

The Bank of Heaven

In Egypt, the wealth of the nation was created from existing material, but in the wilderness, wealth was created from the Bank of Heaven (the mind of God). The currency of the Bank of Heaven, as stated earlier, is God's Word–His thoughts. What Israel would learn, and what we must learn, is that wealth, ultimately, is the in mind. Wealth first begins in the mind of God, and is then transferred into the mind of men through ideas, thoughts, and words. Again, wealth is the ability to assign value. God gives man the ability to assign value by giving him His ideas, His thoughts, and His words.

Let's be clear on the power of God's Word. God's Word is not a powerless divine wish or proclamation. His Word is a creative force. Remember that all creation is the product of God's Word. "By the word of the LORD the heavens were made, and all the host of them by the breath of His mouth. For He spoke, and it was done. He commanded, and it stood fast" (Psalm 33:6, 9). The Bible is clear that God's Word is not just divine vowels and consonants spewed from the mouth of God, but a reality. God never says anything that won't at some point materialize. When God speaks a word, it's accomplished, it's finished, it's done. "So shall My word be that goes forth from My mouth; it shall not return to Me void, but it shall accomplish what I please, and shall prosper in the thing for which I sent it" (Isaiah 55:11). So when God places an idea in the mind of a man, it is a reality waiting to materialize. It is God's gift for subduing the wilderness.

In the wilderness, Israel discovered that human beings, in and of themself, are incapable of creating thoughts; that while we are given the ability to think thoughts, God alone is the originator of them. Simply put, without God there are no ideas, there are no thoughts. This is a concept many in this age of enlightenment find difficult to accept. God's sovereignty over thoughts takes power out of the hands of humans.

It strips all of us of pretense and power. It makes us beholden and dependent on the One who creates and distributes ideas. Thoughts, ideas, and words are created from nothing. I purport that since God is the only One who can create "ex nihilo" out of nothing, we must confess our dependence upon Him. Thought creation is the prerogative of God alone; therefore, not even the devil can create thoughts. Even the devil is beholden to God and is resigned to stealing the thoughts of God, distorting them, then using them for his own nefarious purposes. In creation and restated in the wilderness, God declares Himself to be the source of all wealth. From the mind of God, the Bank of Heaven, comes all wealth.

Sabbath And The Wilderness

There is a parallel between the Sabbath and the wildness. Both are places void of work and free from human effort. They both are places where total dependence upon God is required. Sabbath and the wilderness are places where God is the focus. "You open your hand and satisfy the desire of every living thing" (Psalm. 145:16). In the desperation of the desert, we have no other place to turn but to God. While Sabbath is not a place of desperation, like the wilderness, it is the place where God expects total dependence on Him as reflected in the ban on Sabbath work.

"Observe the Sabbath day, to keep it holy, as the LORD Your God commanded you. Six days you shall labor and do all your work, but the seventh day is the Sabbath of the Lord your God. In it you shall do no work: you, nor your son, nor your daughter, nor your male servant, nor your female servant, nor your ox, nor your donkey, nor any of your cattle, nor your stranger who is within your gates, that your male servant and your female servant rest as well as you" (Deuteronomy 5:12-14).

These places of solitude act as a call to adherence to the Law of Dependence. In the wilderness, as in the Sabbath, both serve as a means of captivating and cultivating the mind to comprehend the economy of God and receive currency from the Bank of Heaven. Israel had to learn, like we must learn that wealth is the product of ideas and ideas come only from the mind of God—the Bank of Heaven.

The wilderness and the sovereignty of God over thoughts are vital concepts in a topsy-turvy global economy. Economists, politicians, and pundits struggle to find answers to the increasingly complex economic woes around the world. The world has become a wilderness desperate for God's intervention. It's a time to be still and know that God is God. It's a time for us to re-evaluate our value system, a time to tap into the economy of God. It's time to worship God.

It was during a time of a topsy-turvy Egyptian economy when Moses requested of Pharaoh. "So Moses and Aaron come to Pharaoh and said, 'Thus says the Lord God of the Hebrews: 'How long will you refuse to humble yourself before me? Let my people go, that they may serve (worship) Me" (Exodus 10:3). Egypt had been devastated by the plagues which had totally destroyed the Egyptian economy. Israel would learn and Pharaoh was forced to concede, economic freedom for Israel and the economic stability of Egypt were tied to worship. Pharaoh and the Israelites were compelled during the economic downturn in Egypt, that resulted form Pharaoh's disobedience to the Law of Dependence, to focus on God as the source of all wealth. They were forced to evaluate their value of the true and living God and their need of the resources totally under His control.

Often, it is not until we are in the wilderness, that we see the need of worship. Until the desert, we are too busy working to stop for worship. We don't see the link between wealth and worship. We are unaware of the fact that in the presence of God we gather Ore Wealth and that it is from Ore Wealth all of material wealth is created. Our self-sufficiency trumps God's sufficiency leading us to elevate work and devalue worship.

The J. C. Penney Story

Consider, for example, this compelling story. "In the midst of the Great Depression, one of America's leading businessmen sank into a personal depression of his own. Now in his fifties, James Cash Penney (founder of the American department store JC Penney) had already built an empire of dry goods stores, dedicated to following the Golden Rule as a basic commercial principle. But when the economy caved in during the 1930s, Penney lost nearly everything–including his health.

His parents had instilled in him a basic Christian faith that had given him the principles on which he had based his life and his business, yet now that faith was being tested. "I was at the end of my rope," he said later. "My business had crumbled, my communications with colleagues had faltered, and even my

... wife and our children were estranged from me. It was all my fault." He was even contemplating suicide.

An old friend convinced him to enter a sanitarium {Battle Creek Sanitarium was owned and operated by Sabbath Keepers} in Battle Creek, Michigan. The rest and medical attention did him good, but there was another event that restored him spiritually. One morning he awoke too early for breakfast and was wandering the corridors when he heard a hymn he remembered from childhood.

> Be not dismayed whate'er betide,
> God will take care of you.
> All you need he will provide,
> God will take care of you.

Following the sound, he stumbled upon a chapel filled with worshiping doctors and nurses. Someone read a Scripture passage: "Come unto me all you that are heavy laden, and I will give you rest." It was a moment of clarity for the hard-working entrepreneur. He had been striving all his life to honor God with his business, but now it was time to rest in the Lord's grace. "At that time something happened to me which I cannot explain," he said later. "It was a life-changing miracle, and I've been a different person ever since. I saw God in His glory and planned to be baptized and to join a church."

Over the next twelve hours, he experienced a kind of conversion. "Suddenly needing to be heard, I cried inwardly, 'Lord, will you take care of me? I can do nothing for myself!' ... I felt I was passing out of darkness into light." The words "only believe" came to him. It was no longer about his own efforts, but God's. "In the midst of failure to believe, I was

CHAPTER FOUR *The Bank of Heaven* — 73

being helped back to believing..."

In the years following his epiphany in that hospital chapel, Penney spoke often of that experience. He talked about the mistakes he made in trusting success rather than God."[6]

The concept of the sufficiency of God is often best learned in the desert when human resources are no longer accessible, when we have exhausted human effort and we are faced with a waterless wilderness. What I have discovered is that a waterless wilderness produces fear for those who are accustomed to living by sight.

"Then all the congregation of the children of Israel set out on their journey from the Wilderness of Sin, according to the commandment of the LORD, and camped in Rephidim; but there was no water for the people to drink. Therefore the people contended with Moses, and said, "Give us water, that we may drink." So Moses said to them, "Why do you contend with me? Why do you tempt God?" And the people thirsted there for water, and the people complained against Moses, and said, "Why is it you have brought us up out of Egypt to kill us and our children and out livestock with thirst" (Exodus 17:1-3).

Fear of death filled the minds of the Israelites much like many during times of financial or economic distress. If we will worship God in our waterless wilderness, God will teach us how to access His unlimited reserves. He will supply us with new ideas that can turn deserts into desirable gardens, waste places into a watered oasis, and impossibilities into possibilities. God doesn't want us to worship Him for what we can receive, but when we worship God we will receive.

Sabbath observance and the wilderness were designed by God to emancipate man from dependence on this world. In the wilderness, God proved to Israel that they could survive and succeed without the economy of Pharaoh. Sabbath observers prove over and over again that one can cease from working for a 24-hour period to worship God and still prosper. They have come to understand that wealth is in your worship, not in your works.

Wealth It's In Your Mind

It's really difficult for twenty-first century people to believe the concept that ideas create wealth, not things. We have been sold a bill of goods that goes like this, "It takes money to make money." No, it takes ideas to create money. What the wilderness and the Sabbath reveal is that things are the creation of ideas. One of the most significant points in this book is: *wealth is in your mind.* Follow me in this sequence of thinking. Wealth comes from ideas. Ideas originate from God. Therefore, we need the time with God that Sabbath and the wilderness provide to receive His ideas and understanding on how to manage and create from God's ideas. It's in spending time with God that we learn how to access the Bank of Heaven.

My wife and I made a decision several years ago, based on our understanding of the Bible, to live a debt-free life. This placed us in the position of using credit as a last option in handling financial matters. At that point, our old Lincoln Town car decided to fall apart. In fact, on what became its final out-of-town trip (we kept the car for another three years while we

CHAPTER FOUR *The Bank of Heaven*

got out of debt), the car broke down two hundred miles away from home. The repair estimate was $1,000.

We had $600 in our checking account, and we had not finished paying all our bills. We knew that once the bills were paid, even the $600 would be depleted. Adding to this dilemma, we had only a small reserve, surely not enough to pay for the auto repair bill.

Since my wife and I had made the commitment not to borrow, we decided to completely trust God for the money. Experiences in our earlier years of marriage had taught us that God could be trusted. As we balanced our checkbook, we knew humanly speaking, that our checking account could not absorb a $1,000 auto repair bill. We were prepared to borrow if necessry, but we were determined to wait on God. To our delight, as we entered the last of the checks, which included the check for $1,000, our account still showed a balance of $175. We were sure there was no miscalculation in our checking account. We didn't have room in our budget for mistakes, so we made sure the checkbook stayed balanced to the penny at all times. There wasn't a banking error or generous benefactor either. God had made a miraculous deposit, from His economy, into our checking account. This was proof to us of the Bank of Heaven.

How do we access the Bank of Heaven? First understand that God wants you to access His bank. He wants you to think His thoughts after Him. He wants to give you ideas that will bless the world through you. "For I know the plans I have for you, declares the Lord, plans for welfare and not for evil, to give you a future and a hope" (Jeremiah 29: 11). Accessing the

Bank of Heaven requires two actions. First, a tithe of time.

"If you turn back your foot from the Sabbath, from doing your pleasure on my holy day, and call the Sabbath a delight and the holy day of the Lord honorable; if you honor it, not going your own ways, or seeking your own pleasure, or talking idly; then you shall delight in the Lord, and I will make you ride on the heights of the earth; I will feed you the heritage of Jacob your father, for the mouth of the Lord has spoken" (Isaiah 58:13, 14). One full 24-hour period of time with the Creator of the universe once a week naturally results in powerful idea transfers from the Bank of Heaven. Second, a tithe (10 percent) of our created wealth. God instructed Israel to return ten percent of their increase as a tangible evident of their dependent on Him and recognition of His ownership of all things. This act of giving would result in unbelieveble blessings. The command was simple, "Bring the full tithe into the storehouse, that there may be food in my house. And thereby put me to the test, says the Lord of hosts, if I will not open the windows of heaven (the Bank of Heaven) for you and pour down a blessing until there will be no more need" (Malachi 3:10). Sabbath and tithe are centered in worship. Both are tangible acknowledgments of God as the source of all wealth. Tithing and the observance of Sabbath are public confessions that one believes, wealth is in your worship not your works.

The McNeilus Family's Story

Denzil D. McNeilus and his family learned early in busniness the benefits of Sabbath observance and tithing. "My

CHAPTER FOUR *The Bank of Heaven*

father started a business called McNeilus Truck & Manufacturing in the early 1970s. Throughout many years of hard work and the Lord's blessings the company flourished. McNeilus Truck & Manufacturing became incorporated with McNeilus Companies, a privately held family business.

In our first years the primary business was the manufactory of concrete-mixer bodies. Our company was considered in ninth place out of nine manufacturers. My father, with strong conviction {about Sabbath observance}, incorporated tithes and offerings into the operation of the company. At the start of the business we were able to give these {tithes & offerings} only at the company's year end. Throughout the year we tried to give to various project of needs.

Soon, as a family, we felt impressed to do more. With much thought, prayer, and careful consideration we took a step of faith and decided to change our system of giving. We decided that, for every individual concrete mixer and mixer truck sold, the company would give a specified amount to the church. We committed to this plan, and our business grew far above our expectations. So we doubled the amount we had initially set. Our company grew again. We again doubled the amount given.

As the company continued to grow and diversify, we developed new products. Our first priority on any new product was to decide what our tithe and offering for that item would be. So as the company grew, so did the amount we gave to the Lord's work. When we eventually sold the company we were the largest concrete-mixer manufacturer in the world.

We believe that God blessed our company and families

so that we may continue to support the Great Commission. I can't begin to list all the blesseings. God watched over us and blessed us with good health so that were able to work the long days needed. He bleassed us us with patient, faithful spouses who support us through good and hard times. He blessed us with healthy, beautiful children born to us or entered our lives through adopton. But most important, He blessed us with the honor of being used by Him. As God continues to blesss us in our various work, we are committed to deepening our stewardship relationship with Him."[7]

Memory Card

"Worship to God has always been of a higher order than work. Remember, man's first full day on the planet was a worship day, not a workday. God grounded wealth creation in worship. True worship is centered in relationship building: God with man, man with God. This was an intentional act of God, so that man would forever understand that true wealth is a gift that results from worship, not work."

- Dr. Roland J. Hill

CHAPTER FIVE
Wealth: It's in Your Worship

There is a battle going on in the West between wealth and worship. And it's sad; it appears that worship is losing. Many spend more time working than they do worshiping. An hour of worship juxtaposed against 40-plus hours of work each week un-abashedly shouts out that work is more important than worship. Why? Because many believe that work is a guaranteed road to wealth and that worship is a roadblock to it. There is the attitude that worship is solely a spiritual encounter, an "other world experience." Worship is seen as totally irrelevant to this world and the struggle to succeed financially. And regrettably, the church has done very little to disavow this misconception. The truth is, the church has fostered and encouraged the battle between wealth and worship. In my book, *Wealth Without Guilt,* I chronicle the 1,500-year lie that ignited this war in the Christian church and how the church has helped fuel this battle between wealth and worship even today. For fifteen hundred years the church taught the non-biblical ideology that money is evil and making money is a sin. This erroneous teaching came out of the Greek philosophy of Gnosticism. This unscriptural concept that teaches that there were two opposing gods that created the world: the material world created by an evil god, and the spirit world created by a good god. Gnosticism created two opposite responses to wealth. There were those who totally abandoned wealth and wealth creation. Many took an oath of poverty, believing that a life in poverty was a higher calling and a more sacred form of worship. On the other hand, there were those who totally abused wealth and wealth creation. This group believed that God is unconcerned about the material world. They believed that their relationship to the material world had no relationship to their spirituality. Therefore, wealth to them was used simply to feed their carnal nature and lifestyle. They believed that the way they obtained their wealth had nothing to do with God. Wealth for them was only about securing for themselves comfort and security.

At the beginning of creation God made clear His view of wealth and worship. Regarding wealth, the created material world, God "saw that it was good," (Genesis 1:25). Worship also was not only good but holy, "So God blessed the seventh day and made it holy, because on it God rested from all his work that he had done in creation" (Genesis 2:3). "Work six days, The seventh day is a Sabbath, a day of total and complete rest, a sacred assembly" (Leviticus 23:3). Worship to God has always been of a higher order than work. Remember, man's first full day on the planet was a worship day, not a workday. God grounded wealth creation in worship. True worship is centered in relationship building: God with man, man with God. This was an intentional act of God so that man would forever understand that true wealth is a gift that results from worship not work. This concept was made clearer to me as I studied Isaiah 58:13-14. In this passage the seed promise for prosperity is discovered. Here is where God reveals the relationship between wealth and worship. Growing up observing the Sabbath, it was a family tradition every Friday evening to open the Sabbath with this passage. And even as an adult, I have continued to

CHAPTER FIVE *Wealth: It's in Your Worship* 83

repeat this precious promise. But like many Sabbath observers, I missed the prosperity pledge. It's disheartening but true; I saw the Sabbath simply as a day of rest and worship, but never as a promise of prosperity. I guess many of us who observe the Sabbath have been so fixated on the misconceptions about wealth, a result of Gnosticism, that it has prevented us from seeing the promise of prosperity offered through the Sabbath.

The promise of Isaiah 58:13 begins with a call to worship. It's a call to give God adoration and praise. This wealth-building text details the acts in preparation of worship. No work, shows respect for God's command. No involvement in sports, politics, or personal plans, is designed for focus on the relationship. No engaging in secular conversation keeps the focus on God and God alone.

Worship today is mainly about the individual. There is little concern about God. The question for most worshippers is, "What's in it for me? How can I benefit?" Worship for most has become a duty, it's that plain and simple. "Let's give God His one hour, get what we can get, and off to work we go," is modern man's mantra. But Isaiah's prosperity passage draws us away from self into a deeper relationship between the Creator and His creation in the context of worship. Sabbath worship was designed by God for man. It is a time for man (us) to delight ourselves in the presence of God, a time to spend with the God of love. Here is the Orthodox Jewish view of the Sabbath, "The meaning of the Sabbath is to celebrate time rather than space. Six days a week we live under the tyranny of things of space; on the Sabbath we try to become attuned to holiness in time. It is a day on which we are called upon to share in what is eternal in time, to turn from the results of creation to the mystery of creation, from the world of creation to the creation of the world."[8]

The struggle with worship, dedicating a 24-hour period of time to God, is evidenced by the frantic need to work in order to create wealth. Wealth creation is not seen as a gift, but a reward or pay. Therefore, the Sabbath command is not seen as an emancipation document but an unofficial certificate of enslavement. Many miss that this 24-hour period of worship was designed by God to free our minds from the idea that we must earn our way to personal salvation and success. It is a time to refresh our thinking and practice of the Law of Dependence. What this Isaiah passage conveys is that this intimate time with God results in wealth creation. This uninterrupted time in the presence of God results in a spiritual high. In this heightened relationship experienced in worship, the worshipper experiences the fullness of God's joy and grace. "You make known to me the path of life; in your presence there is fullness of joy; at your right hand are pleasures forevermore" (Psalm 16:11). This worship experience cultivates the human mind for the currency of heaven: God ideas, God's thoughts, God's words. And in this mindset, the promise of the Sabbath can be fulfilled.

Sabbath is a sign of the covenant between God and man. "Moreover, I gave them my Sabbaths, as a sign between me and them, That they might know that I am the Lord who sanctifies them" (Ezekiel 20:12). Israel understood that the covenant between God and man was not just expressed in the cessation of work as a response to worship, but through a tangible wealth transfer that results from the relationship. "You shall remember the Lord your God, for it is He who gives you the power to get wealth, that He may confirm His covenant that He swore to your fathers, as it is this day" (Deuteronomy 8:18). This wealth transfer is expressed in this promise found in Isaiah 58:14 by the words, "I will feed thee with the heritage of Jacob's father." What was the heritage promised to Jacob? Seven gifts were pledged to Jacob as a result of true Sabbath observance: holiness of character; the blessing of health; superior intellect; skilled in agriculture and animal husbandry; superior craftsmanship; unparalleled prosperity; and national greatness.[9] Notice that these are all gifts given, not rewards earned. It was God's intent to bless Israel to the point where people would ask, "How did you get your incredible wealth?" And the response would be, "God gave it to us as a gift for worshipping Him." This was no lame, wishful thought for worshippers to ponder, but a reality spoken by God Himself. "for the mouth of the Lord has spoken" (Isaiah 58:14).

The struggle to worship by entering the Sabbath rest is in reality a struggle of belief–the struggle to believe that man is not the captain of his own ship, that God is the source of life and wealth, and that man must ultimately look to God for wealth creation. There is in all of us that inner struggle to believe that there is a personal God who cares enough about us to take care of all our needs. "Casting all your anxieties on Him, because He cares for you" (1Peter 5:7). And that's just the point of this Holy Time called Sabbath. It is a time of revelation about God. True worship allows us to see God as the Almighty God, the all-knowing God, the eternal God, and the Creator God.

What I've come to understand is that our beliefs about wealth and wealth creation are directly tied to our view of God and our view of God is directly tied to our worship of God. It is in worship that we confess Who is the source of all value. In worship we are reminded of our value to God. Only in worship are we reminded that we are created in the image of God; we did not evolve; God personally created us. This *Holy Time* with God becomes a weekly reminder of the gift of assigning and allocating value on inanimate and animate objects that results in the creation of wealth. What I have discovered is that Sabbath worship brings life into perspective. Sabbath helps us to understand that God is valued above all, that God values us, that He gives us the ability to give value to things, and that things can only have value in relationship to God and man.

Wealth Without Worship

But there is an irony that occurs when material wealth is void of worship. The irony goes like this; God gives us the power to give value to things, so we give value to those things, then as we pride ourselves in the things we've given value to, we turn away from the God who gave us the gift of giving value! Soon we are accumulating things as a means of giving us value. It does not make any sense, but we do it anyway. Understand, we lose our sense of value when we turn away from the worship of God.

Jesus captured the dangers of wealth without worship in this text, "The seed cast in the weeds is the person who hears the

Kingdom news, but weeds of worry and illusions about getting more and wanting everything under the sun strangle what was heard, and nothing comes of it" (Matthew 13:22). In a parabolic way, Jesus placed us on notice. He warned us that there is an allurement about wealth when it is detached from worship. In this text, Jesus gave us the sense that material wealth can be mesmerizing. Wealth without worship is dangerous because it has the potential of becoming animated by demonic spirits. Moses and Aaron encountered this in Pharaoh's palace when the Egyptian magicians caused their sticks to become snakes (see Exodus 7:8-12).

"The magicians did not really cause their rods to become serpents; but by magic, aided by the great deceiver, they were able to produce this appearance. It was beyond the power of Satan to change the rods to living serpents. The prince of evil, though possessing all the wisdom and might of an angel fallen, has no power to create, or to give life; this is the prerogative of God alone. But all that was in Satan's power to do, he did; he produced a counterfeit. To human sight the rods were changed to serpents. Such they were believed to be by Pharaoh and his court. There was nothing in their appearance to distinguish them from the serpent produced by Moses."[10]

Wealth detached from God becomes an alluring power. It mesmerizes many to believe that happiness can be found in things. It hypnotizes many to believe that love and acceptance can be found in luxurious living. It captivates many to believe that security can be found in the accumulation of stuff. It charms people with the idea that value and self-worth can be found in material wealth. And ultimately, it convinces many to believe that eternity (a peaceful life) can be found in wealth creation. Please don't miss this: when the worship of God is forsaken, the power of things becomes irresistible. "No servant can serve two masters, for either he will hate the one and love the other, or else he will be loyal to the one and despise the other. You can not serve God and mammon" (Luke 16:13). In Jesus' warning about material wealth, He chose the word mammon. He intentionally personified material wealth as a god or spirit. In reflecting on the words of Jesus I've concluded, for the purpose of this book, that mammon is material wealth animated by demonic spirits. Spirits of lust, envy, manipulation, greed, control, addiction, deception, etc. often enter into the mammon dynamic. For me, the only explanation for the accumulation of things in an illusive and illogical attempt to find value and self-worth in the twenty-first century is a mesmerizing force–mammon. The reality is that many have been deceived by wealth. Many have contracted *affluenza*. Affluenza is a painful, contagious socially transmitted condition of overload, debt, anxiety, and waste resulting from the dogged pursuit of more. It is the bloated, sluggish, and unfulfilled feelings that result in the tireless effort to keep up with the Joneses (an idom referring to the comparison to one's neighbor as a benchmark for a standard of living). It is the unsustainable addiction to wealth creation for the purpose of finding self-worth.[11]

What I have discovered is that affluenza is the stray mark of distorted values. Rather than finding our value in God, we search for value in things. Distorted values are the consequence of disconnecting from the source of real value. Therefore, the only cure for affluenza is true worship. Only in true worship are we reconnected to the source of true significance. Worship is the antidote for affluenza because it moves us away from self. It moves us away from the horizontal view of keeping up with the Joneses to a vertical view of God. Worship fills our minds with the glow of God's glory, thereby, dimming the value of earthly things. As God renews our worth in worship, so then is our sense of value renewed. We begin to see ourselves as God see us–valuable. We are reminded in true worship that there is no such thing as a self-made man. There are only God-made men, bound by the Law of Dependence. True worship is a confession of our position before God; creatures dependent upon Him.

What I have discovered is that Sabbath worship was designed by God to be a bulwark against affluenza. As Israel prepared to entire the land of promise, which would be a place of prosperity, God cautioned them against the danger of material wealth.

"Beware that you do not forget the Lord your God by not keeping His commandments, His judgments, and His statutes which I commanded you to day. Lest–when you have eaten and are full, and have built beautiful houses and dwell in them; and when your herds and your flocks multiply, and your silver and your gold are multiplied, and all that you have is multiplied; when your heart is lifted up, and you forget the Lord your God who brought you out of the land of Egypt, from the house of bondage…then you say in your heart, 'My power and the might of my hand have gained me this wealth" (Deuteronomy 8:11-14, 17).

God set aside 82 days of the year that included 30 days

of feasting and 52 weekly corporate worships as Sabbaths where work was forbidden and worship required. These were times to remember God, the source of all life and wealth. Clearly, from the Sabbath requirements, God set worship at the heart of the nation and worship as the foundation of wealth creation. To stop work for nearly one-quarter of the year was public proof that their security was in God's sovereignty and not man's work. Their worship was evidence of their belief that wealth is a gift from God.

The Wealth Test

Wealth (money) is man's greatest test of worship. Again, Jesus set wealth (money) in juxtaposition to the worship of God. "No servant can serve two masters, for either he will hate the one and love the other, or else he will be loyal to the one and despise the other. You cannot serve God and mammon" (Luke 16:13). In this text, Jesus positions money as the acid test. He makes it clear that man's true character will always be evidence by the way he uses, creates, manages, and values money. Jesus stated, "For where your treasure is, there your heart will be also" (Matthew 6:21). Wealth and worship are in a constant battle–and this conflict is at the heart of the war between the forces of good and evil, God and Satan. This battle could be no more evident than in the life of Jesus Himself. His first major conflict at the beginning of His public ministry was between worship and wealth. It was over what Jesus valued most. "Again, the devil took Him to a very high mountain and showed Him all the kingdoms of the world and their glory. And he said to him, 'All these I will give You, if You will fall down and worship me.' Then Jesus said to him, Be gone, Satan! For it is written, "You shall worship the Lord your God and Him only shall you serve," (Matthew 4:8-10). Satan postured himself as the great benefactor. His battle cry was, "If you worship me, I will give you." Satan understands what few are willing to believe, that wealth is a gift. It is true, Satan can and does give wealth. But note: since he can't create and can only copy, the wealth he gives is at best counterfeit or at worst stolen. Ponder this point: wealth is never solely the product of work. It is either a gift from God or a gift from the devil. That's very difficult to digest in an age of self-made men. We really believe work is our road to wealth creation and that hard work will earn wealth. But it is important to ponder this truism that wealth is a gift. This profound prophetic point prods us to examine the source of wealth offered. The reality, as seen in Jesus' temptation in the wilderness, is that the devil can give wealth and often disguises his gift of wealth in hard work. He deceives us to believe we earned it. Then, Satan leads us to self-worship all the while believing that "My power and the might of my hand have gotten me this wealth" (Deuteronomy 8:17). Work becomes our place of worship, consuming our time, energy, and affections. We began to value work more than God because work is believed to provide us temporal treasures. We value job, career, and business acumen above worship because "stuff" becomes our savior. Wealth for many is not the allocation or assignment of value, but simply the accumulation of material possessions. This distorted view of wealth blinds us to our true potential for wealth creation. I hear the distorted view from some of those who attend my seminars.

"Do you have wealth?" is the legitimate question asked by those who have heard my presentations. Their question is really like the famous lines in the movie *Jerry Maguire*; "Show me the money!" I don't have an overabundance of things – neither do I seek to inspire others by the display of wealth or the accumulation of riches. What I know from years of prayer, Bible study, research, and observation, is that when the focus is mainly on material possessions as a sign of wealth, one does not understand what true wealth is. Satan uses this distorted view of wealth as a means of tempting us to prove our wealth in outward display. Look at Jesus' personal battle with Satan over wealth in the wilderness. There was no outward evidence that Jesus was the Son of God, the source of all wealth. He was very likely dirty and smelly, seemingly alone, and emaciated from hunger. Here was the wealth and worship challenge: "If you are the Son of God, turn these stones into bread." "If" is an expression of doubt. "If you are wealthy, then show me," was Satan's challenge. Jesus was tempted to display His divinity.

The temptation to display one's wealth is just as real as Jesus' temptation to display His divinity. Our ability to create wealth is part of our divine gifting. So the enemy tempts us saying, "If you are wealthy then why aren't you living in a mac-mansion? If you are wealthy then why aren't you driving a Bentley? If you are wealthy then where are your designer clothes?" Satan's tantalizing inquiry continues, "You say you are the child of the King; then where are your large bank accounts, extensive investments, and vaults of gold and silver?"

Jesus' response to the wealth challenge is an example

for us about wealth display. He did not give a verbal response to the challenge. Why should Jesus respond to that which He knew? His divinity was part and parcel of who He was and is. If Jesus were to have given in to the enemy's request for display, it would have been a denial of who He was. Jesus understood that the need to display wealth is a recipe for a dangerous lifestyle. Once we respond to the enemy's request for outward display, we start a vicious race, with a constantly-changing finish line that ends in death to the victim. True worshippers resist the temptation to display their wealth because they understand, like Jesus, that displaying one's wealth is evidence they don't have it.

Avoiding the display of wealth is difficult because our materialistic society encourages opulent lifestyles. The simple life isn't valued, appreciated, or rewarded. The result is a society with the philosophy that says, "Make all you can; save all you can; and then sit on the can." While this philosophy is rooted in John Wesley's wealth creation philosophy, it is often misquoted and misunderstood. John Wesley's quote , "Make all you can; save all you can," was really a call to responsible living. He encouraged worshippers to use their God-given talents to create wealth and live a simple and frugal life so that they could give extravagantly to the Kingdom of God for the betterment of society.

Why must wealth be tied inseparably to worship? Our sinful natures are so weak, the pull of riches is so strong, and the temptation to parade our prosperity is so intense, that worship is our only safeguard. Sabbath rest and a life centered in worship keep life and wealth in perspective. The weekly pilgrimage to the Sabbath mine reminds us who God is—Creator/Owner; reminds us who we are—creatures/stewards; reminds us that we owe all of our worth, wealth, and life to God; and reminds us that wealth is truly in our worship, not our works.

Memory Card

"Ore Wealth is the creative ember of God in every man that ignites His image in us. It's that part of man that transcends human sense perception. It's man's original wealth-creation component. It's an implanted element of the mind of God. Ore Wealth is the base element of all wealth creation that comes from the mind of God. But it is not God. Ore Wealth is God's ideas, God's words, God's thoughts, but not God Himself."

- Dr. Roland J. Hill

CHAPTER SIX

You are Job

"Go to school, get a good education, so you can get a good ____." Filling in the blank is automatic, it's part of our subconscious mind, it's engrained in the fabric of Western philosophy, and it's a lie. Going to school may get you a good education, but school will never guarantee a job. In fact, you were not created to go get a job; you were created to be the job. You were created to create. You were born with the desire and the ability to prosper. "The desire to accumulate wealth is an original affection of our nature, implanted there by our heavenly Father for noble ends."[7] God placed you on the planet to create wealth for the expansion of His Kingdom and the betterment of humanity.

Wealth Defined

Wealth is a context-dependent term; therefore, let me be clear about wealth in the context of this book. Wealth, for this discussion, is defined in two ways: Ore Wealth and material wealth. Ore Wealth is the creative ember of God in every man that ignites His image in us. It's that part of man that transcends human sense perception. It's man's original wealth-creation component. It's an implanted element of the mind of God. Ore Wealth is the base element of all wealth creation that comes from the mind of God. But it is not God. Ore wealth is God's ideas, God's words, God's thoughts; but not God Himself.

Ore Wealth is a gift on loan to us from God. Since Ore Wealth is God's ideas, thoughts, and words, it does not need physical manifestation to be considered a reality or visible presence to validate its existence. Ore Wealth is ever existing in the mind of God. Even when Ore Wealth is transferred to the mind of man, it never needs to be displayed to validate its existence. In simple terms, God's ideas are real—just because they are God's ideas.

Material wealth, on the other hand, is Ore Wealth made visible. It originates from the hand of God or the hand of man. It is ideas turned to products, patents, services, copyrights, and material things that have been given value by man. It is tangible and touchable, but temporary. Material wealth is available for use in everyday life, but since it is created, it can be destroyed. It exists at the behest of God or man. That's why we can never place faith and hope in material wealth. "Do not toil to acquire wealth; be discerning enough to desist. When your eyes light on it, it is gone, for suddenly it sprouts wings, flying like an eagle toward heaven" (Proverbs 23: 4-5).

Ore Wealth

Ore Wealth is given at birth, but is nurtured, cultivated, and ignited in worship. As mentioned earlier, it is in worship that God transfers His ideas and His thoughts. Worship is both a corporate experience and a private practice. It is being in intimate communion with God. It is in this state of mind that Ore Wealth transfers take place. Again, Ore Wealth is a gift to be used, but never owned. It is on loan from God.

CHAPTER SIX *You Are Job*

Few understand the power of Ore Wealth and material wealth. Ore Wealth is a divine gift, loaded with divine power. These ideas, words, and thoughts fueled by divine power are capable of producing enormous good or catastrophic evil. When Ore Wealth is detached from God, it is dangerous and deadly. Therefore, Ore Wealth, if not harnessed in worship, will ignite the combustible sin in us and around us, causing forest fires of destructive products, services, patents, and copyrights. Please understand, Ore Wealth is so powerful that if it is not managed properly, it will become a god. God Himself spoke of the power of Ore Wealth in His statement about the antediluvians (people before the flood), "If as one people speaking the same language they have begun to do this, then nothing they plan to do will be impossible"(Genesis 11:6). Ore Wealth is an awesome gift distributed by God without partiality but with the understanding that weekly worship, as a place of debriefing and reminder, is required. The weekly pilgrimage to the Sabbath mine replenishes our confidence and conviction about what true wealth is. It strengthens our commitment to only use Ore and material wealth to the glory God and for the benefit of humanity. True worship enables us to stand victorious in the battle over material display.

Alexander was one of my wife's students in a middle school where she taught several years ago. When he discovered that I am an author, he emphatically declared, "Dr. Hill, you are rich, your husband is an author."

My wife quickly corrected him, "No, Alexander, I am not rich."

"But, Dr. Hill, you are rich, and what are you doing

teaching here?"

After thinking about the implications of Alexander's statements, my wife then responded, "You are right Alexander, but I am not rich, I am wealthy." My wife reflected on our Ore Wealth of God-ideas that has been turned into books, CDs, and videos that have funded portions of our ministry and benefited thousands worldwide. Understanding the difference between Ore Wealth and material wealth eliminates the need for outward display. It releases the stress of keeping up with the Joneses. And it allows us to answer the call of a simpler life free from clutter. Knowing the difference between Ore Wealth and material wealth engenders confidence in us about wealth production in any situation in life.

My friend, Dr. Leroy Moore, a professor of theology and religion, recounts growing up with little material wealth, but with an enormous amount of Ore Wealth. He confessed to me that there were many days he went to school without breakfast or lunch and wasn't sure about supper when he arrived home from school.

"We were really poor," stated Dr. Moore, "but my godly mother would say every day, 'We're rich, we're rich, we're rich." She refused to allow their lack of material wealth to overshadow their Ore Wealth. This mother's belief, the result of Bible study and private and corporate Sabbath worship, produced children who have all become productive professionals and who have blessed the world with their contributions, spiritually, socially, and financially. True worshippers never determine their wealth by the size of their bank accounts, cars, houses, or investments. They understand that earthly value systems are fickle; what is

CHAPTER SIX *You Are Job*

considered of value today could easily be worthless tomorrow.

In testimony before the Ways and Means Committee of the United States Senate in 1921, George Washington Carver spoke of his faith and the part it played in his success as a scientist and inventor. A senator asked:

"Dr. Carver, how did you learn all of these things?"

Carver confidently and quickly answered, "From an old book."

"What book?" asked the senator.

Carver replied, "The Bible."

"Does the Bible tell about peanuts?"

Carver answered, "No sir, but it tells about the God who made the peanut. I asked Him to show me what to do with the peanut, and He did."[12]

George Washington Carver, who is credited with the creation of hundreds of products from peanuts, soybeans, and sweet potatoes, confirmed the reality of Ore Wealth. What is exciting, securing, and comforting about Ore Wealth is that you may lose all of your material wealth and still be wealthy. This is clear from the story of Job (read about it in Job 1-3).

According to the biblical account, Job was the wealthiest man in the east. His wealth: "7,000 sheep, 3,000 camels, 500 yoke of oxen, and 500 female donkeys, and very many servants, so that this man was the greatest of all the people of the east" (Job 1:3). As a true worshipper, Job understood the temporary nature of material wealth; therefore, he intentionally placed his relationship with God above his material wealth. But as stated earlier, there is a battle between wealth and worship, and Job found himself caught in the crossfire. Satan confronted God with the accusation that Job only worshipped Him because of the material wealth. "Then Satan answered the LORD and said, 'Does Job fear God for no reason? Have You not put a hedge around him and his house and all that he has, on every side? You have blessed the work of his hands, and his possessions have increased in the land. But stretch out your hand and touch all that he has, and he will curse You to Your face" (Job 1:9-11). Amazingly, God stepped aside, dropped the hedge from around Job's material wealth, and allowed the instantaneous destruction of all his material wealth. Notice Job's response at the loss of all his material wealth. "Then Job arose and tore his robe and shaved his head and fell on the ground and worshiped. And he said, "Naked I came from my mother's womb, and naked shall I return. The LORD gave, and the LORD has taken away; blessed be the name of the LORD" (Job 1: 20-21). Worship was at the center of Job's life, therefore, in loss, his first response was to worship, not to worry. In his wilderness, Job confessed God as the benefactor of all his material blessings and willingly submitted to God's will for having wealth or losing wealth.

If you are having a Job experience right now, stop and check your worship experience with God. If your worship is on track, make this declaration, "Since I have a relationship with God, I still have Ore Wealth, and since I have Ore Wealth, I am wealthy." Remember, if you lose your job and all your material possessions, you haven't lost your ability to create more material wealth. The only way to lose access to all true wealth is by disconnecting from God through neglecting worship.

Occupation

I write about Ore Wealth because I understand how difficult it is to remain positive and hopeful in a hopeless world. Having studied wealth creation principles for more than three decades, I know that the only real hope for the unemployed in this new global economy is through an understanding of Ore Wealth. Unemployment is not a joke, as I expressed in my groundbreaking book, *Theo-Economics: Unlocking the Wealth Potential of Individuals and Nations*. I wrote this a decade-and-a-half ago as I watched the world economy changing, "When we talk about unemployment in this country, what we see are facts, not faces. We think of plants, not people. We hear numbers, not names. But unemployment is about people–real people. People who could very well be your next-door neighbor. They could be relatives and friends. Or–maybe even you. But no matter who it strikes, unemployment is devastating."[13]

The good news is that you don't have to be unemployed. Sabbath worship is a promise of full employment. "Six days you shall labor, and do all your work" (Exodus 20:9). At the beginning of the fourth commandment God offers a promise by giving a command. He mandates work as a prerequisite for worship. While work doesn't create wealth, it is part of the evidence that God has given us the gift of wealth. Human effort is proof of our belief in a sovereign God. For the true believer, work is not an option; it is an obligation.

Israel, like so many today, was faced with the challenge of adhering to God's work mandate due to the place of the command; it was given in the wilderness. There were no jobs in the wilderness. How could God mandate work without jobs? What Israel would come to understand is that, "As the will of man cooperates with the will of God, it becomes omnipotent. Whatever is to be done at His command, may be accomplished in His strength. All His biddings are enablings."[14] The Sabbath commandment is God's statement of responsibility. God holds Himself responsible for our obedience to His six-day work mandate. The six-day workweek, then, is predicated on divine intervention, participation, and empowerment. But notice, the command was not to get a job, but to work. This work mandate wasn't a call to get a job, but to be a job. God fulfills His work mandate in us by giving us occupations rather, than jobs.

What is an occupation? An occupation is talents bestowed, abilities divinely implanted; it's God's individual divine wiring given to all people at conception. When I talk about occupation, I share my own story. At the tender age of six I gave my heart to Christ and accepted my call to ministry. I was called to be a pastor and that's what I am. Truthfully speaking, that's all I have ever wanted to be. God wired me in my mother's womb to be a pastor. At conception, He gave me the gifts of preaching, teaching, and writing as tools for my occupation so that I could obey His command, "Six day you shall labor." My occupation is a gift. I didn't earn it. I don't deserve it, but I will say that I am required to develop it. You, too, have been wired from conception with an occupation. But honestly, it's difficult for most people to accept their life calling. Having a job is what most people know. Being chained to what my wife calls a "W2" is all most people can imagine.

CHAPTER SIX *You Are Job*

Israel had become shackled with the job mentality before God delivered them from Egyptian bondage. They went into Egypt with occupations, but ended up with jobs. In that foreign land they were forced to surrender their occupations and acquire the trade of brick masonry. Their work was to build pyramids and palaces for Pharaoh. It was a job with very little fulfillment and no real benefits for the masses. The only purpose for the brick-making trade in Egypt was to display material wealth and glorify the gods of stone, iron, nature, and ultimately, the god of self. Many today, in this turbulent economy, like the Israelites in Egypt, derive very little fulfillment or real personal benefit for their jobs.

Jobs are modern day brick-making. Often the requirement on these jobs, like Israel in bondage, is to make bricks without straw. Many who in the past have become contented or paralyzed with jobs are now wondering about their future in this unstable global economy. What we are faced with today is the fact that employment in this new global economy hinges on this biblical question, "What is your occupation?" (Genesis 46:33). What I see as one of the greatest challenges in a postindustrial society is discovering one's occupation. Knowing one's occupation or vocation is more vital now than perhaps ever before. As traditional means of making money are diminishing and various types of jobs have become obsolete, many will be forced to search frantically for work. That's why I believe the question of occupation is vital to the success of individuals, churches, communities, and ultimately nations.

Discovering your occupation is an exciting and empowering experience. Your occupation is in the DNA coding for fulfilling your role in society and the Kingdom of God. It is your birthright. Occupation is a person's God-gifting. Joseph understood how crucial occupation was to freedom and worship. So as he extended the invitation for his family to move to Egypt to live during the famine, he gave these instructions, "When Pharaoh calls you and says, 'What is your occupation?' you shall say, 'Your servants have been keepers of livestock from our youth even until now, both we and our fathers,' in order that you may dwell in the land of Goshen, for every shepherd is an abomination to the Egyptians," (Genesis 46: 33-34).

As prime minister of Egypt, Joseph understood that the Egyptian economy was not concerned about the development of true wealth or the empowering of the masses. It was only concerned with the worth and wealth of the privileged. The masses were seen only as a means to create wealth. On the other hand, Joseph's family had long lived in the economy of God. Their fortunes and future were not tied to land or possessions but to the guidance and provisions of the unseen God. It was clear to Joseph that his family's destiny was inextricably tied to obedience to the Law of Dependence. Therefore, Joseph anxiously counseled them to preserve their economic edge and financial freedom by safeguarding their occupation. Joseph further understood that their occupations were protected only as they continued their worship of the true and living God.

Unfortunately, Israel allowed herself to be lured into idol worship, which ultimately resulted in the loss of her financial edge. Egypt didn't have to be a place of slavery for Israel. But when Israel stopped worshipping God, Egypt seduced her and ultimately enslaved her. On a personal note, if you stop worshiping God, you will lose your sense of identity. You will become blinded to your occupation and enslaved by a job. I see it happening to the masses all over the world. Able-bodied people are reduced to paupers and slaves by human systems that give them jobs or make them feel worthless without a job. Here's one for you: J.O.B. stands for "Just Out of Brains." God never intended for the greatest of His creation to check their brains at the door of a job. Ponder this question, "What is your occupation?"

Sheepherding was the occupation of Joseph's family as they settled in Egypt. As shepherds, they did not depend on the economy of other nations. They depended on the God who watered the fields and protected the flocks. But as they were forced from the fields to the city to work for Pharaoh, they lost their God-calling. But God, in His mercy, would not allow His chosen people to be chained forever with Egyptian jobs. So He delivered them, led them to the wilderness, and gave them new occupations, so they would learn again how to depend upon Him. Interestingly enough, they were given their new occupations to equip them for work on the first corporate project out of slavery: building a place of worship for God. God's work mandate was followed by an assigned project. "Let them build me a sanctuary so that I might dwell among them" (Exodus 25:8). Retooling this new nation would be centered in worship.

In the wilderness God would call them to new occupations. "The LORD said to Moses, 'See, I have called by name Bezalel the son of Uri, son of Hur, of the tribe of Judah, and I have filled him with the Spirit of God, with ability and intelligence, with knowledge and all craftsmanship, to devise artistic designs, to work in gold, silver, and bronze, in cutting stones for setting, and in carving wood, to work in every craft. And behold, I have appointed with him Aholiab, the son of Ahisamach, of the tribe of Dan. And I have given to all able men ability, that they may make all that I have commanded you'" (Exodus 31:1-6).

In His miraculous bestowing of gifts and talents on Israel, God advanced the idea that the primary purpose of all vocations and occupations is to bring glory to God in service to His Kingdom. Israel's new occupations were to be used to serve a new King. In the wilderness God trained them to be Godpreneurs: craftsmen, tradesmen, and herdsmen who would trust God for their own businesses. And as Godpreneurs, God would teach them that, even in the wilderness, there was potential for prosperity. In the wilderness there was plenty of work to do to fill the needs of the new nation. Filling the needs of this great multitude of people would be the model for wealth creation for the nation.

God teaches us, in the story of Israel, that there is no excuse for a non-productive life. "God has equipped man with the capabilities needed to fill his special place. To every individual God has assigned a place in His great plan,"[14] so they would have the ability to obey His work mandate. When I talk about occupation or vocation, I'm talking about a gift of God from birth or a gift of God bestowed after being reborn in Christ. God created us with our unique set of gifts and talents and "the specific station in life appointed for a man is determined by His capabilities."[15] Every occupation was given with the purpose of work. Work would become God's method of outsourcing His creative power. God has the ability, without the help of man, to supply the needs of all His creatures, but He graciously extends to us the opportunity to use our occupations to meet the needs of others. That's what He taught Israel in the wilderness, that their wealth creation was tied up in supplying the needs of others inside the nation. The needs of the new nation of Israel were great: priests to fill spiritual needs; tentmakers to fill housing needs; herdsmen to fill clothing needs; and farmers to fill food needs. As they learned to supply the needs among their own people and in service to God, they would be prepared to service the needs of others outside of the nation. Wealth creation is about filling needs and creating value to help eliminate the woes and needs of others.

What needs do you see that you can meet in your community? Understand, you add value (create wealth) by fulfilling needs. There is a reciprocity of value that goes on in communities among responsible people. As you meet needs in a community through your occupation or vocation others meet your needs through their occupations. That's the cycle of true wealth creation.

Discovering Your Occupation

How do I discover my occupation? I say emphatically that discovering your occupation begins with worship. In the presence of God the mind is enlightened: you begin to sense your uniqueness and calling. Worship provides the atmosphere for honest evaluation of oneself. It opens the mind and unclogs the ears to better see God and hear His voice. What I have discovered is that in worship one learns the importance of meditation, not the mystical meditation, but the contemplative thoughtfulness that sits quietly awaiting God's revelation. Meditation becomes the medium for the transfer of ideas, first about oneself, then about one's gifts, and finally ideas that will answer needs.

In meditation ask yourself this question, What am I naturally good at doing? What comes easiest for me to do? And finally, What do I have a passion for doing? I'm amazed at how many hesitate when it comes to accepting their natural gifts and talents. But I guess I shouldn't be amazed because all of us have a natural tendency to want to be like someone else. We want to have the gifts and talents that others have, so we devalue our natural gifting and go in search of some exotic gift we see in others. Reality check: you are what you are. Accept it. Your unique toolbox of gifts and talents is what God gave you to create wealth.

At one period in my life I became desperate about making a living. I had worked for many years in my occupation but I still wasn't making the kind of money I felt I needed to make. Mind you, all my basic needs were being met, but I had become anxious about what I felt I needed. So I started filling out job applications. Up to that point in my career, I had only filled out two or three job applications and I did this before I finished college. After about a half-dozen applications, some with negative responses, others with no response, I found myself getting depressed. In my moment of despair, God spoke to me, "I gave you three talents: preaching, teaching, and writing. Those are the ones I want you to use to create wealth. You don't need a job. You need to trust Me." Let me clarify my perspective about working a job. A job is work that may or may not have anything to do with your gifts or talents. It's just work to make a living. Most of us have been forced, at some point in life, to take a job just to survive, and honestly, I see nothing wrong or demeaning about it. In fact, God often uses jobs to build character and teach us skills that we may not have learned otherwise. What I also found to be true is that there are many who work in their occupation on a job. They love their work, they are working in their God-calling, so in reality, it isn't a job. People who are in this category tend to see their employer as their major client, not their boss. Remember, "God has equipped man with the capabilities needed to fill his special place. To every individual God has assigned a place in His great plan."[16]

Wealth creation doesn't come by accident or happenstance. And those who accept and walk in their God-calling discover that God has a wealth creation process. Walk back with me into the Sabbath mine; here God clearly defines His method for creating wealth.

But before we investigate the seven steps of God's wealth creation process, let me reiterate this important point: wealth is not what I acquire, but what I create by adding value. This truism supplements the definition of wealth, which is the allocation and assignment of value. "I do nothing to get wealth – I am; therefore I have." This is not hocus-pocus or mystical thinking. First and foremost, the statement is recognition of who we are and what we are. We are God's creation, created in His image. Secondly, there is a confession about our dependence on God. We have no value apart from God; therefore, any value that we create is really God's value flowing through us. Hence, we are obligated to obey to the Law of Dependence for the creation of any wealth. And finally, it is an acceptance of the power that God has given human beings to add value to the visible world.

Understand, God's wealth creation process is never about achievement, recognition, or accumulation; it is about the celebration of the work of God in one's life. Therefore, get-rich-quick schemes aren't appealing, nor is wealth display desired. God's wealth creation process is primarily about bringing glory to God and blessing humanity. Understanding this is key to creating wealth God's way.

God's Wealth Creation Process

STEP 1 - *God starts His wealth creation process with heaven-born ideas.* Remember that ideas are the currency of the economy of God. God rarely bestows material substance to produce material wealth. He gives us ideas as a means of producing wealth. What I have discovered is that heaven-born ideas lock us into dependence on God. They are the linchpin in the Law of Dependence. What's clear is that the wealth creation process cannot start until God gives us the ideas. As mentioned before, we do not create ideas, ideas are created from nothing and only God can create from nothing. Yes, it is true that there are those who create wealth apart from God. But those ideas used to create wealth were really God's ideas stolen by the devil and them planted in evil men's minds and used for evil purposes. Check your ideas to make sure they come from God.

STEP 2 - *God channels His ideas through one's God-given gifts and talents.* Seldom, if ever, does God give ideas for wealth creation outside of one's occupation. God, in normal circumstances, will not give anyone ideas about nano technology to someone who doesn't have scientific ability. I am amazed at how many people who are duped into pursuing wealth creation in areas in which they have no gifting. The belief of many is that there are only a few ways to build wealth and that property is one of them. The truth is that there are literally thousands of honest, legitimate, God-inspired ways to make money. There are as many ways to make money as there are different talents and gifts. I have talked with real estate brokers and have read about those who own lots of property. And I have discovered that for most, it was not the property that made them money. It was the ideas centered on their gifts and talents and put into the marketplace that created wealth for them. Property was just a by-product of making money. Real estate, for these people, is simply a repository for their wealth. Avoid any ideas for wealth creation that are outside of your gifts and talents, unless God directs you otherwise.

STEP 3 - *Make your ideas concrete.* Ideas are useless if they are never made concrete. God never gives ideas for them to just lay dormant. Since we are outsourcers of God's creative work, He always gives ideas to meet needs. Needs are met when ideas are turned into visible, useable wealth. Concrete ideas come in various forms: products, services, patents, and copyrights. Therefore, concrete ideas don't just happen; they require study, work, and seeking God. God just doesn't give us the ideas and leave us to create wealth alone. He actively guides the entire wealth-creation process. "Thus says the Lord, your Redeemer, the Holy One of Israel: 'I am the Lord your God who teaches you to profit, who leads you in the way you should go'" (Isaiah 48:17). Notice the process: God gave the children of Israel the ideas, talents, or gifts, then the plan for developing the idea, and the power for building the Tabernacle. The Law of Dependence makes clear that God is needed in every phase of wealth creation. In God's wealth creation process, there will never be a place to brag about what we have done. "For by grace you have been saved (created wealth) through faith. And this is not your own doing; it is the gift of God, not a result of works, so that one may boast" (Ephesians 2:8-9).

STEP 4 - *Find a real need and fill It.* God's wealth-creation process was never designed to indulge. It was never designed to prey on man's carnal nature. It was never designed to create needs in mankind. Instead, God's wealth creation process was designed to allow human beings to share in the care and stewardship of the creation. He created us to be helpmeets to others on the planet. While God gave the helpmeet status to women, I believe that the principle of shared responsibility was also implied for all human beings. No one person can take care of all of his needs; therefore, we look to others to help meet our real needs. Real needs are things essential for life as opposed to felt needs, those things that only appear to be necessary for life. I discovered that true wealth creation is sustainable. It always meets real needs: food, clothing, housing, education, health care, energy, and encouragement.

STEP 5 - *Formalize and legitimize your business.* God's wealth-creation plan recognizes the place of ruling powers. "Let every person be subject to the governing authorities. For there is no authority except from God, and those that exist have been instituted by God" (Romans13:1). A formalized business becomes a place of witness and restriction. It's a place of witness to non-believers about God's power to build, prosper, and sustain a business. But it is also a place that holds a business accountable for its actions. Here are two basic types of formalized business: non–profit or not-for-profit, and for profit, which are formed through a sole proprietorship, partnership, or corporation.

STEP 6 - *Plan your work and work the plan.* The process is incomplete if there is not a strategy to place the idea into the marketplace. Writing a clear business plan and then executing the plan is essential to accomplishing the vision. While work doesn't create wealth, there is no wealth without work. "So also faith by itself, if it does not have works, is dead" (James 2:17).

STEP 7 - *Trust God as a Godpreneur.* God's wealth-creation process is a call to Godpreneurship. What is Godpreneurship? Godpreneurship is in the business of creating wealth by using God's methods, means, and mind. The Godpreneur is a business man or woman who has been given a vision by God to fulfill a specific need through a formalized business. Godpreneurs are mission-driven with one purpose–to bring glory to God. They are worshippers who are motivated and inspired by God to create wealth for the Kingdom. They never see themselves in competition with others but are simply fulfilling their place in society. Godpreneurs view and manage their businesses with God as the owned, thus they totally trust in God for its success. For the Godpreneur wealth creation is viewed as a form of worship.

When Stanley Tam became a Christian, he was determined to live out its true meaning. As a young man struggling to make a go of business during the Depression, he committed to allowing God to guide his actions. Slowly, he reaped success in his businesses, first in silver recover, then in plastic manufacturing. Although it was difficult for him, he felt the call to witness about Jesus to his contacts. He even followed God's leading and had his lawyer draw up legal papers making the Lord his business partner, that was until January 1955.

In January of 1955, Stanley and his wife Juanita visited Ecuador, Peru, Brazil, and Colombia. They were moved as they observed the work of missionaries sharing their testimonies with missionaries and Latin Americans. While in Medellin, Colombia, Stanley spoke to a small crowd. The Holy Spirit's presence was strong. Although the appeal had not been emotional, many people came forward to pray. But Tam found he could not sit down, he was in deep thought. He later explained why he couldn't sit down, "For I came once again into a milestone encounter with God," he said.

CHAPTER SIX *You Are Job*

God asked him, "What is the most important thing in all the world to you?" Tam looked down at the altar. "To see people seek Your face, Lord, as a result of the Holy Spirit's blessing upon my testimony," he replied.

"Stanley," God said, "If a soul is the greatest value in all the world, then what investment can you make that will pay you the greatest dividends a hundred years from now?" Tam was already giving sixty percent of his income and much of his time. What was God asking him to do? He realized God was asking him to become His employee. "An employee, Lord? Isn't that what I am now?" he asked. "We're partners now, Stanley. I want you to turn your entire business over to me." Stanley was stunned. "I can't go back to Ohio and turn my business over to you," he told the Lord. "Isn't sixty percent enough? Many Christians don't so much as give you ten percent." The Lord reminded him of the parable in Matthew 13:45-46. "The Kingdom of Heaven is like unto a merchant seeking goodly pearls, who, when he had found one pearl of great price, went and sold all that he had, and bought it." Tam was convinced. On that day, January 15, 1955, he told God that he would turn the entire business over to him. Stanley Tam would no longer even be a stockholder in the company. His committment has paid off. Stanley Tam's business is still producing for the Kingdom.

As Tam noted, when a man seeks to involve God in the center of his life, he can expect divine encounters. Often they will run counter to our personal interests (Read Stanley Tam's full story in his book, *God Owns My Business*).

GOD'S WEALTH-CREATION CHART

Step 1	*Heaven-Born Ideas*
Step 2	*God-given Gifts & Talents*
Step 3	*Concretized Ideas*
Step 4	*Find a Need*
Step 5	*Write a Business Plan*
Step 6	*Formalize the Business*
Step 7	*Trust God - Godpreneur*

Memory Card

"The Divine Law of Attraction is a force exhibited when one's will is aligned with God's will, as a result of true worship, a holy allurement occurs that attracts unexplainable favor to accomplish the mission of God for one's life."

— Dr. Roland J. Hill

CHAPTER SEVEN
The Divine Law of Attraction

Have you wondered why some people seem to always get the breaks and you don't? Does it bother you that some people seem to succeed against all odds and you, on the other hand, face failure at every turn? Do others know something you don't know? Is there a secret that's been kept from you? I've pondered this concern a great deal over the past forty years and have come to the conclusion that, yes, there is a secret and regrettably, it's been hidden away in plain view. It's the secret of worship. Through distortion and centuries of misinformation about worship, many have missed the deep secrets about life and wealth creation that are locked up in worship. So the question is, What is worship? Let me begin by saying what worship is not. Worship is not an order of service that drives a corporate religious gathering. Worship is not religious rituals done to appease God. And finally, worship is not metaphysical meditation to center oneself in the universe. While worship may contain an order of service, involve religious ritual, and does require meditation (focusing one's mind on God), at its core, worship is much broader and deeper. Worship is a God encounter. It's the time where one becomes saturated with the Divine. It's the time where the *Holy Glow* is ignited and the *Divine Magnetism* is activated. This type of God encounter is mystical and powerful, but seldom experienced by most. That's why I believe many of us have relegated worship to one to two hours per weekend and maybe 10 or 15 minutes a day.

The Numinous Experience

Walk with me once again deep into the Sabbath mine while we examine the phenomenon of true worship. The German theologian Rudolph Otto wrote about what he termed the numinous experience. The numinous is what happens when one comes into the presence of the Almighty. It's a mysterious occurrence that defies human reason. Words are useless to express this God encounter. The numinous is the unexplainable experience of worship. And what is worship? Worship is standing, bowing, and being prostrate in the presence of Yahweh, much like Isaiah's experience after King Uzziah's death. "In the year that King Uzziah died I saw the Lord sitting upon a throne, high and lifted up; and the train of his robe filled the temple. Above him stood the seraphim. Each had six wings: with two he covered his face, and with two he covered his feet, and with two he flew. And one called to another and said: "Holy, holy, holy is the LORD of hosts; the whole earth is full of his glory!" And the foundations of the thresholds shook at the voice of him who called, and the house was filled with smoke. And I said: 'Woe is me! For I am lost; for I am a man of unclean lips, and I dwell in the midst of a people of unclean lips; for my eyes have seen the King, the LORD of hosts!' Then one of the seraphim flew to me, having in his hand a burning coal that he had taken with tongs from the altar. And he touched my mouth and said: Behold, this has touched your lips; your guilt is taken away, and your sin atoned for'" (Isaiah 6: 1-7).

All throughout this book, my desire has been to move you to a place of true worship. "Surely you have granted him eternal blessings and made him glad with the joy of your presence" (Psalm 21:62).

For me, reflecting on Isaiah's experience and my own, worship is an intimate experience with the Creator that takes place throughout the day for six days, but finds its apex on Sabbath. True worshipers become divinely saturated in Sabbath worship; they become fully engaged with God. It is during that worship encounter, deep in the Sabbath mine, that we are reminded of our creatureliness and our dependence on God. Isaiah voiced the humbling effects of true worship, "Woe is me! For I am lost; for I am a man of unclean lips, and I dwell in the midst of a people of unclean lips; for my eyes have seen the King, the LORD of hosts!" (Isaiah 6:5). In true worship, there is a deflating of ego and self-sufficiency. In the presence of a Holy God, our creature consciousness cries out, "I am nothing in the presence of that which is all." There in worship, a devaluation of self takes place, and a recognition of God as the source of all value is provoked. We sense in the presence of God that we are valueless apart from Him. "I am the vine, you are the branches. Whoever abides in me and I in him, he it is that bears much fruit, for apart from me you can do nothing" (John 15:5). Could this be why many hesitate to spend time in God's presence on the Sabbath? Could it be this fear of facing the reality that there is no value, thus no wealth creation, apart from God? Wow! Yet, when confronted with our creatureliness and accepting our total dependence upon God, that's when the Divine Law of Attraction is activated. As we reach out to God and are saturated with this God encounter, an unexplainable phenomenon happens. True worship is like standing in the Texas summer heat. Imagine what would happen if you were to stand in the Texas heat for 24 hours. I can assure you something would happen. You would bake, fry, and maybe even die. You can't stay in the Texas heat without something happening. The same holds true in the presence of God. Weekday worships keep us connected, but the 24 hours spent with God on the Sabbath sets us aglow. There is a Holy Glow that results from extended periods with God, as verified in the life of Moses. "When Moses came down from Mount Sinai, with the two tablets of the testimony in his hand as he came down from the mountain, Moses did not know that the skin of his face shone because he had been talking with God. Aaron and all the people of Israel saw Moses, and behold, the skin of his face shone, and they were afraid to come near him" (Exodus 34:29-30).

In the presence of God we are filled with His *Being*, creating a magnetic force field that enshrouds us and ignites the Divine Law of Attraction. What is the Divine law of Attraction? It is a universal law that is impartial but personal. It works in the life of true worshipers everywhere and under all circumstances. Though it is impartial, this universal law works uniquely for every person according to God's plan for his or her life. The Divine Law of Attraction is a force exhibited when one's will is aligned with God's will, as a result of true worship, a holy allurement occurs that attracts unexplainable favor to accomplish the mission of God for one's life. But this law doesn't work alone. It works in tandem with the Law of the Harvest that states: "for whatever one sows, that will he also reap" (Galatians 6: 7). God's drawing power, His favor, combined with our human effort, becomes The Divine Law of Attraction. This universal law is a gift of divine allurement that draws into the life resources (material, human, and heavenly) needed to accomplish God's mission for the life.

Operation — The Divine Law of Attraction

How does the Divine Law of Attraction operate? In worship, one is saturated with God's effervescent glory, that glory blends in with ones gifts, talents, and character, creating a magnetic energy. This human/divine combination produces an irresistible force field that draws favor from God and man. "As the will of man cooperates with the will of God, it becomes omnipotent. Whatever is to be done at His command may be accomplished in His strength. All of His biddings are enablings."[17] Let's be clear, The Divine Law of Attraction is really God working through man to accomplish His purpose. It's what I call the *Paradox of Production*, which states that what man produces looks like all man's doing, but on closer examination one realizes it is all God's doing. What is evident in the Divine Law of Attraction is that *the doing is by God and for God*. The purpose in this universal law is not to give security, surplus, or salvation to mankind, but to bring glory to God and a revelation of who God is to the world. "That you may know that I am the Lord your God" (Ezekiel 20:20). "Let your Light so shine (Divine Law of Attraction) that men may see your good works and glorify the Father in Heaven" (Matthew 5:16).

While the Divine Law of Attraction is a divine magnetic energy, there are three confessions that are essential for its activation. First, the acknowledgement of God as the source of all life and value. Second, a willingness to acknowledge total dependence on God as evidenced in a weekly 24-hour work-free worship day. Third and finally, a commitment to develop and use one's gifts, talents, and resources for the mission of God.

The Divine Law of Attraction is not hocus pocus or does it bring about a utopia. I say this because of man's carnal nature that would lean toward a surface understanding of this universal law, which could lead some to seek to apply it for unhealthy reasons. For example, some will be attracted to The Divine Law of Attraction out of fear. This law provides answers for them to their worry about poverty (financial woes), position (social status), and posterity (their future). Others would look to this law as a means of finding value. This universal law does give power. It gives an individual the ability to control, to a certain extent, people and circumstances, which, in turn, allows one to feel valuable because one can be in control. And then there are those who quickly grab hold of this law for selfish purposes. In their attempt to be the center of their own world, they would use this universal law to make everything and everyone revolve around them. Let's be clear–God does not make the Divine Law of Attraction available for any of the above reasons.

The Divine Law of Attraction does not imply or encourage the idea of a life free from challenges. As mentioned, in the presence of God, where this universal law is activated, ego and sufficiency are overshadowed and the mission of God becomes paramount. Remember, the law is not about what we do but

CHAPTER SEVEN *The Divine Law of Attraction*

what God does. The Divine Law of Attraction does release God's favor and man's favor, but it is not favoritism. A selfish desire for favoritism covets favor without restrictions or obedience in search of a care-free life. The Divine Law of Attraction, on the other hand, draws favor as a result of obedience. This universal precept is not for the faint of heart. While it attracts favor, it does provoke disfavor. Favor is released in three ways. First is Divine Favor. Divine Favor is God's gracious protection, provision, and presence given to accomplish His mission for our lives. It's His divine allurement that creates a magnetism that opens the way for the second favor, human favor. What few seem to understand in the twenty-first century is that there is no such thing as a self-made man. Every person is trained, nurtured, and sustained in community. We were not designed by God to go at life or our mission in life alone. We need the help of others. As the Divine Law of Attraction is activated, it draws people to us to help accomplish God's mission. Joseph, the eleventh son of Jacob, best illustrates the Divine Law of Attraction.

"The LORD was with Joseph, and he became a successful man, and he was in the house of his Egyptian master. His master saw that the LORD was with him and that the LORD caused all that he did to succeed in his hands. So Joseph found favor in his sight and attended him, and he made him overseer of his house and put him in charge of all that he had. From the time that he made him overseer in his house and over all that he had the LORD blessed the Egyptian's house for Joseph's sake; the blessing of the LORD was on all that he had, in house and field. So he left all that he had in Joseph's charge, and because of him he had no concern about anything but the food he ate" (Genesis 39: 2-6). From Potipher's house, to the prison, and finally to Pharaoh's palace, this divine magnetism drew heavenly and human resources to accomplish God's mission for his life (read Joseph's story in Genesis 37 - 47).

But just as this universal law draws favor, it draws disfavor. There is a battle waging between the forces of good and evil and it is seen played out as true worshippers experience success and create wealth for the Kingdom of God. "Then the dragon was furious with the woman and went off to make war on the rest of her offspring, on those who keep the commandments of God and hold to the testimony of Jesus" (Revelation 12:17). This Divine Law of Attraction draws haters. "Now Joseph had a dream, and when he told it to his brothers they hated him even more" (Genesis 37:5). Joseph attracted the favor of God, Potipher, and Pharaoh, but he drew the disfavor of his brothers. Note: as the favor of God and man is seen in your life, anger will be provoked in the hearts of some. Understand, that as prosperity and success is experienced by you, a true worshipper; the anger of others will be fueled. Their question will be, "How can you succeed and prosper working fewer hours and taking a 24-hour worship break once a week?" As I have said, this universal law is not for the faint of heart. Haters become inflamed when they see you succeed with limited talents, pedigree, and connections. They become furious because you succeed without compromising your worship. Let me be clear, the Divine Law of Attraction comes at a price and few really want to pay it. But I assure you: it's worth the price, whatever the cost.

The Divine Law of Attraction guarantees success because

true worship always results in wealth creation. It is absolutely impossible to experience a full day of Sabbath rest and a life centered in worship in the presence of God without the Divine Law of Attraction being ignited, resulting in wealth creation. True worshippers will create wealth. There is no such thing as non-productive worshippers. If you are a true worshipper, prepare for God's gift of wealth. The question, then is not whether or not I will have wealth, but How shall I live as I create wealth?

The Power of Wealth

In a society that sees little connection between worship and wealth the question "How shall I live with wealth?" is seldom discussed. The assumption is made that since we created it, it belongs to us; therefore, we are free to do with it as we please, no questions asked. Ultimately, we don't ask the question because we don't see wealth as a gift from God. We don't see ourselves as stewards of the wealth, but owners of it. What's alarming is that we are totally unaware of the power of wealth. We take ownership over power we have no idea how to handle; power that God never intended for us to own, just to manage.

Wealth is power and the evidence of this power is seen in the use and abuse of it. We see it in politics, the pulpit, and the pew. The president of a religious organization was presented with a challenge from a wealthy congregant. "I will give you $40,000 cash, if you will arrange to move my pastor," were the words of this irate well-heeled parishioner. The deep-pocketed member was using what I call, "money muscle." That's the kind of abuse we're facing more and more in an affluent society. Let's be clear: wealth isn't evil, it's just dangerous. There is nothing evil about the Bugatti Veyro Super Sport with it's aluminum, narrow Angle 8 Liter W16 Engine with 1200 hp that gets up to speeds of 267 mph, and goes from 0-60 in 2.4 seconds. But driving it is dangerous. So it is with wealth. Wealth is so powerful that God gives warnings about its use.

"'Take care lest you forget the LORD your God by not keeping His commandments and His rules and His statutes, which I command you today, lest, when you have eaten and are full and have built good houses and live in them, and when your herds and flocks multiply and your silver and gold is multiplied and all that you have is multiplied, then your heart be lifted up, and you forget the LORD your God, who brought you out of the land of Egypt, out of the house of slavery, who led you through the great and terrifying wilderness, with its fiery serpents and scorpions and thirsty ground where there was no water, who brought you water out of the flinty rock, who fed you in the wilderness with manna that your fathers did not know, that he might humble you and test you, to do you good in the end. Beware lest you say in your heart, 'My power and the might of my hand have gotten me this wealth'" (Deuteronomy 8:11-17).

The Warning About Wealth

God's warnings are crucial because the danger of wealth is so real. As wealth increases, for many, worship decreases and they lose sight of God. Wealth without worship then becomes an intoxicant and we are tempted to say like King Nebuchadnezzar, "'Is not this the great Bablyon which I built by my might and my power as a royal residence and for the glory of my majesty'" (Daniel 4:30). We become arrogant with our affluence, self-sufficient with success, and wicked with the wealth. And since we struggle with the regulation that worship brings, and we live in a society that worships the god of self, fueled by an economy built on indulging self, we end up destroying self. Check the high rates of suicide among the rich and affluent. Look at the records for drug abuse, alcoholism, and addictions of various kinds among the affluent. It's evident that wealth without worship is deadly.

God, in concern and care for His creation, opens to us the Sabbath mine: "Remember the Sabbath day to keep it holy" (Exodus 20:8). This weekly pilgrimage to the Sabbath mine is a reminder that God is the source of all wealth, that man's wealth creation has limits, and wealth is not determined by one's work but by a relationship with God in worship. Rabbi Abraham Joshua Heschel writes this about Sabbath: "In the tempestuous ocean of time and toil there are islands of stillness where man may enter a harbor and reclaim dignity. The island is the seventh day, the Sabbath, a day of detachment from things, instruments, and practical affairs as well as of attachment to the {S}pirit."[18] It's a time where one becomes saturated with the divine, igniting the Holy Glow and activating the Divine Law of Attraction. God's plan for true worshippers is for them to leave the Sabbath with a confidence of knowing that success is simply for the asking. He wants believers to begin praying the prayer of Eliezer, "'O Lord, God of my master Abraham, please grant me success today and show steadfast love to my master Abraham'" (Genesis 24:12). This is the prayer of success Eliezar learned living in the home of Abraham. It's a prayer I will expound upon later in my next book, *The Prayer of Eliezer: It's Bigger Than Me*. Just know that those who commit to the true worship of God will begin to glow. The Divine Law of Attraction will begin to work for you and God will bring into your life everything needed for your success.

Shabbat and The Glow

There was a wise worker bee named Shabbat who lived far away in a busy beehive. Shabbat was known throughout the bee world for her unusual work schedule, long life, high production of honey, and her unique glow. Every evening at sunset Shabbat would climb into her cell, fold her wings, and go to sleep, while all the other bees worked through the night. Not only did Shabbat rest each evening, she completely stopped working for 24 hours one day each week. On that day, Shabbat would fly away to a secret place and would not return until the day was done. For 24 hours Shabbat could not be found.

"Good morning everyone. It's time to start the day!" Shabbat bugled, buzzing joyously as she fluttered around the hive prepared to start a new week of gathering pollen.

"Why is she so happy?" Solis protested. "No one can be happy every day." Solis' irritation could no longer be hidden.

"And look at her, she's glowing like the sun," retorted Mercuri, as she shielded her eyes from the intense radiance of Shabbat's tummy.

"Shabbat, can you please cover up?" Iovis pleaded, squinting from the brightness radiating from Shabbat's glowing belly.

"What's wrong, Iovis?" Shabbat sheepishly answered, totally unaware of her glow.

"It's your abdomen. It's so bright, it's hurting our eyes." Iovis looked around, encouraging the other bees to chide in.

"Yes, please cover up," the entire group chorused.

Shabbat was astonished at the hive's response for she hadn't noticed the glow. She knew she felt good all the time. She knew she always had an abundance of energy, but she didn't know about the glow. That night as she climbed into her cell, just before she folded her wings to fall asleep, Shabbat took out her mirror and looked at her tummy. Sure enough, it was just the way the bees had described it. Her belly was glowing as if the sun was inside of it. Shabbat closed her eyes and went to sleep.

"Good morning everyone. It's time to start the day!" Shabbat bugled, buzzing joyously as she fluttered around the hive prepared to start another day of gathering pollen. But on this day she wore a big scarf to shield the glow. Each night as Shabbat climbed into her cell she examined her tummy. Each day the glow grew dimmer. By the sixth day Shabbat no longer needed to wear the scarf.

"Explain the glow," Lunea whispered after slipping secretly into Shabbat's cell late one night.

"I can't," Shabbat quietly responded. "All I know is that after I return from my time away, it happens. Would you like to go and find out for yourself?" Shabbat continued.

"No, I was just curious, that's all," Lunea twitched as she spoke. Then without saying another word, she slipped quietly back to her cell before she could be noticed.

"Good morning everyone. It's time to start the day!" Shabbat bugled, buzzing joyously as she fluttered around the hive prepared to start another day of gathering pollen. But this was the sixth day, so instead of climbing into her cell and folding her wings and going to sleep as she usually did, Shabbat caught a big gust of wind and fluttered off to her secret place.

"Welcome to your weekly rest," Princess Sabrina graciously greeted Shabbat as she did every week as Shabbat quietly glided to her resting place in the hollow of a purple corn poppy. On the right side of Shabbat, on a beautiful yellow cosmos flower, lay a dozen bees from other colonies. They all greeted Shabbat as family and then fluttered off into the garden sanctuary. As the sun slowly set in the west, Shabbat folded her wings and fell asleep. Early the next morning, as the sun burst over the eastern sky, Shabbat flapped her wings and began her Sabbath rounds. First she floated over by the crystal river that snaked its way throughout the entire garden. Then she skipped across two rolls of pink buttercups laying along the banks of the river.

"Happy rest day," Princess Sabrina broke Shabbat's thoughts. "How was your rest?"

"My rest was wooooonderful," Shabbat blurted out with a smile so big it could have covered the garden.

"I'm glad you rested well. Are you ready for your weekly jaunt?" Princess Sabrina spoke as she positioned herself to guide Shabbat through the enchanted rose garden.

"I can't wait," Shabbat chirped as she eagerly fell in line behind Princess Sabrina as they headed east toward the enchanted rose garden.

"Ooo, wow," Shabbat's mouth fell open as the lavender hollyhock gate to the garden swung open. It was as if this was Shabbat's first time, but it wasn't. She had made the trip to the garden sanctuary for months, but the enchanted white roses were so stunning that each visit overwhelmed her.

"Enter," Princess Sabrina spoke as she ushered Shabbat in. "Drink as much as you like."

Shabbat rolled out her long, tube-like tongue and began sucking nectar out of the white roses. One, two, three, four, five, one hundred, one thousand roses until she had filled both stomachs and was once again glowing like the sun.

"See you next week," Shabbat cheerfully spoke to Princess Sabrina the next morning as she headed back to the hive.

"Good morning everyone. It's time to start the day!" Shabbat bugled, buzzing joyously as she fluttered around the hive, prepared to start another week of gathering pollen.

"I want to go next week," Lunea whispered to Shabbat as they worked side-by-side gathering nectar from a nearby flower.

"Sure, be ready at sunset on the sixth day" Shabbat said. She was pleasantly surprised, but didn't show it.

On the sixth day, just before sunset, Lunea arrived at Shabbat's cell and the two quietly disappeared.

"Welcome to your weekly rest," Princess Sabrina graciously greeted Shabbat as she did every week as Shabbat quietly glided to her resting place in the hollow of a purple corn poppy.

"And who did you bring with you, Shabbat?" queried Princess Sabrina.

"This is my friend, Lunea," Shabbat spoke up proudly, "She's come to experience Sabbath rest."

Early the next morning Shabbat and Lunae began their Sabbath rounds. "Ooo, wow," Lunae's mouth fell open as the lavender hollyhock gate to the garden swung open and she gazed upon the white roses. The two rolled out their long tube-like tongues and began sucking nectar out of the white roses. One, two, three, four, five, one hundred, one thousand roses, until their stomachs were filled and their tummies were glowing like the sun.

On their arrival back from the garden sanctuary, Lunea was charged and changed.

"Good morning everyone. It's time to start the day!" Shabbat and Lunea bugled, buzzing joyously as they fluttered around the hive, prepared to start another week of gathering pollen. It wasn't long before others joined Shabbat and Lunae. As the weeks passed a glow lit up the entire hive. All the bees stopped each evening, climbed into their cells, folded their wings, and fell asleep. On the sixth day, they flew off to the garden sanctuary and returned with glowing tummies; that is, all but six angry bees.

"I hate their glow! And Shabbat, she thinks she's all that," Satania spouted out, her face twisted in an ugly frown. "How can they waste so much time sleeping at night, leaving all the work on us when they go off to their hideout?" She continued, "Shabbat, you've caused all the problems around here," Satania hurled her biting words.

"What do you mean, Satania," Shabbat boldly spoke up. "The hive is producing more honey than ever and no one is complaining except you and your five friends. What's the problem?"

"We can't stand the glow and we can't understand how your production is higher while your work hours are less." Satania pitched her angry words as she huddled with her friends.

"The best way to understand, Satania, is to come with us next weekend," Shabbat spoke in sympathetic tones, hoping to charm Satania and entice her to join the group on the trip to the garden sanctuary.

"No way! I'm not going to let you trick me like you tricked all the others!" Satania's words were filled with poison. "We're leaving the hive today. We're going to a place where people earn their honey." Satania growled as she and her five friends flew away to the unnamed colony in the desert on the east side of Edora.*

The End

*<i>Shabbath and The Glow</i> written by Roland J. Hill

Memory Card

"Our sinful natures are so weak, the pull of riches is so strong, and the temptation to parade our prosperity is so intense, that worship is our only safeguard."

- Dr. Roland J. Hill

CONCLUSION

I spent the first year and a half of ministry after seminary reading motivational books in my spare time and learning about wealth creation. Like so many others, I had the dream of becoming a millionaire by the time I was 35. But becoming a millionaire for me was never about the house, the cars, or the exotic vacations, it was always about resources for ministry. But in my search through all the contemporary wealth-creation philosophies and the works of popular financial gurus, there was always a missing ingredient. Their material would pump me up, but it wasn't long before the air was gone and I was flat again, financially and emotionally. I found myself always buying another book or another audio recording to stay pumped up. My hope and prayer for this book is not to pump you up, but to fill you up with the Word of God. My desire is that you will experience what I experience each time I review the concepts found in this book–a renewal and a refreshing. My plan for this book was never to just pump you up, but to fill you up with God's ideas, thoughts, and words.

If you will simply write out the major concepts in this book on 3" x 5" cards and review them every day, I guarantee you will experience the abundant life. You will experience what I call "crazy favor" as the Divine Law of Attraction goes to work in your life. Let me be clear as I end my time with you. The abundant life is not a life without challenges, failures, and mistakes. Instead, it is life filled with the presence of God, which makes the challenges, the failures, and the mistakes turn out well. "And we know that for those who love God all things work together for good, for those who are called according to his purpose" (Romans 8:28). Remember, you have Ore Wealth in you. You don't need to go out to get wealth; you are wealth. God has given you the gift of creating value; thus you have the ability to create wealth by adding value. Take your talents and turn them into cash understanding that Wealth: It's In Your Worship Not Your Works. This is the secret millions have been searching for through the ages. Please share it with others.

- Dr. Roland J. Hill

GLOSSARY OF TERMS

1. **Bank of Heaven:** the mind of God where all ideas are created and distributed.
2. **Godpreneurship:** the business of creating wealth by using God's methods, means, and mind.
3. **Godpreneur:** a business man or woman who has been given a vision by God to fulfill a specific need through a formalized business.
4. **Life rhythm:** Time–the boundary for work, worship, leisure, rest, and ultimately wealth creation for mankind.
5. **Material wealth:** Ore Wealth made visible. It originates from the hand of God or the hand of man. It is ideas turned into products, patents, services, copyrights, and material things given value. It is tangible and touchable, but temporary.
6. **Occupation:** talents bestowed, abilities divinely implanted, it's God's individual divine wiring given at conception or at rebirth in Christ to all people.
7. **Ore Wealth:** the base element of all wealth creation that comes from the mind of God. But it is not God. Ore Wealth is God's ideas, God's words, God's thoughts; but not God Himself.
8. **The Divine Law of Attraction:** a force exhibited when one's will is aligned with God's will as a result of true worship; a holy allurement occurs that attracts unexplainable favor to accomplish the mission of God for one's life
9. **The Law of Dependence:** the recognition that God is self-existent, eternal, and Creator of everything and by adher-

ing to the Law of Dependence can created beings find true security and created things have value.

10. **The Paradox of Production:** what man produces looks like all man's doing but on closer examination one realizes it is all God's doing.
11. **Theo-economics:** God's unique, distinct, and separate economy. God's philosophy for creating and managing wealth for time and eternity.
12. **Wealth:** the assignment and allocation of value.

ENDNOTES

1. Abraham Joshua Heschel, *The Sabbath*, Farrar, Straus and Giroux, 18 West 18th Street, New York, New York, p. 16.

2. Amasa Walker, *The Science of Wealth*, John Wilson and Son, 1866, pp. 7, 8.

3. Ellen G. White, *Education*, Pacific Press Publishing, Nampa, Idaho, 1952, p. 99.

4. Ronald A. Knot, *Over & Over Again!*, North American Division of Seventh-day Adventist, Sliver Spring, MD, 1998, p. 217

5. Ellen G. White, *Patriarchs and Prophets*, Review and Herald Publishing Association, Washington, D.C., 1890, p. 258.

6. http://www.christianity.com/ChurchHistory/11630672

7. Ronald A. Knot, Over & Over Again!, North American Division of Seventh-day Adventist, Sliver Spring, MD, 1998 pp. 65, 66

8. Abraham Joshua Heschel, *The Sabbath*, Farrar, Straus and Giroux, 18 West 18th Street, New York, New York, p. 26.

9. *Seventh-day Adventist Commentary -Vol. 3*, Review and Herald Publishing Association, Hagagstown, MD, pp. 27, 28

10. Ellen G. White, *Patriarchs and Prophets*, Review and Herald Publishing Association, Washington, D.C., 1890, p. 264.

11. www.theaffluenzaproject.com

12. www.melban.com/his/george-w-carver

13. Roland J. Hill, *Theo-Economics: Unlocking the Wealth Potential of Individuals and Nations*, Helping Hands Press, Duncanville, Texas, 2006, p. 76.

14. Ellen G. White, *Counsels on Stewardship*, Review and Herald Publishing Association, Washington, D.C., 1890, p. 138.

15. Ellen G. White, *Christ's Object Lessons*, Review and Herald Publishing Association, Washington, D.C., 1900, p. 333.

16. Ellen G. White, *Prophets and Kings*, Pacific Press Publishing Association, Mountain View, California, 1917, p. 536.

17. Ellen G. White, *Education*, Pacific Press Publishing Association, Mountain View, California, 1917, p. 267.

18. Abraham Joshua Heschel, *The Sabbath*, Farrar, Straus and Giroux, 18 West 18th Street, New York, New York, p. 29

ABOUT THE AUTHOR

Dr. Roland J. Hill is the director of Development and Stewardship for the Texas Conference of Seventh-day Adventists. He has served as a pastor, professor, and administrator for over 37 years. Dr. Hill is the author of 17 books and is an internationally known preacher, teacher, and lecturer. He and his wife, Dr. Susie M. Hill, have conducted hundreds of seminars worldwide on stewardship, Theo-Economics, and marriage and the family. Dr. Hill is a graduate of Oakwood University, Andrews University, and Reformed Theological Seminary. He has been married to Susie, for 37 years and they have two adult children and three beautiful granddaughters.

Booking Information:

Dr. Susie M. Hill
P.O. Box 380941
Duncanville, Texas 75138
www.helpinghandspress.com

OTHER BOOKS BY HELPING HANDS PRESS

Theo-Economics: God's Wealth System, Unlocking The Wealth Potential of Individuals and Nations by Dr. Roland J. Hill. This book reveals new biblical ways of making, managing and investing money in an economy that is based on God. Deep concepts and easy reading.
$20.00 Paperback

The Financial Fitness Manual by Drs. Roland & Susie Hill. A powerful step by step guide to managing your way out of debt.
$30.00 Workbook and CD

Wealth Without Guilt by Dr. Roland J. Hill. Discover as you read this intriguing book the 1,500-year lie that keeps people from reaching their financial potential.
$4.99 Ebook

The Word on Money by Dr. Roland J. Hill. This is not your ordinary book on money. This book challenges you to think critically about money and the human philosophies that under gird the economy.
$10.00 Paperback

www.helpinghandspress.com